Illustrator
Bruce Hedges

Editor
Mara Ellen Guckian

Editorial Project Manager
Ina Massler Levin, M.A.

Editor in Chief
Sharon Coan, M.S. Ed.

Cover Artist
Denise Bauer

Art Coordinator
Denice Adorno

Creative Director
Elayne Roberts

Product Manager
Phil Garcia

Imaging
Ralph Olmedo, Jr.

Publishers
Rachelle Cracchiolo, M.S. Ed.
Mary Dupuy Smith, M.S. Ed.

Big & Easy Patterns
Themes

Compiled by

Loralyn Radcliffe

Teacher Created Materials, Inc.
6421 Industry Way
Westminster, CA 92683
www.teachercreated.com

ISBN-1-57690-592-6

©2000 Teacher Created Materials, Inc

Reprinted, 2000.
Made in U.S.A.

T ble of Conte..ts

Using the Patterns. 5

Language Arts Patterns and Ideas. 6

　Fountain Pen. 7

　Pencil 8

　Eraser 9

　Alphabet. 10

　Little Miss Muffet. 36

　Humpty Dumpty 39

　The Three Little Kittens 42

　Jack Jumped Over a Candlestick. 45

　Baa, Baa, Black Sheep 46

　Hickory Dickory Dock 49

Social Studies Patterns and Ideas 52

　White House. 53

　Capitol 55

　Eagle 57

　Statue of Liberty. 59

　Liberty Bell 62

　Doctor 64

　Dentist 66

　Mail Carrier 68

　Police Officer 70

　Firefighter. 72

　Fire Hydrant 74

　Teacher 75

　Car 77

　Truck 78

　Bus 80

　Train. 82

　Airplane 85

　Cruise Ship. 87

　Bicycle 89

　Costumes and Clothing of the World

　　Tanzania 91

　　Japan. 93

　　Argentina 95

　　Holland 97

　　Australia 99

　　Play Clothes 101

Table of Contents *(cont.)*

Social Studies Patterns and Ideas *(cont.)*

Cowboy 103
Longhorn Steer 106
Horse 108
Pioneer Boy 110
Pioneer Girl 112
Covered Wagon. 114
Iroquois Female and Infant 118
Iroquois Male 121
Long House 124
Tipi. 128
Pueblo. 130

Science Patterns and Ideas 132
Build a Flower 133
Plant Needs. 136
Sun 139
Wind. 140
Rain 141
Snowflakes 142
Cloud 143
Rainbow 144
Stages of a Butterfly 146
Stages of a Frog 150
Tyrannosaurus Rex 154
Triceratops 157
Apatosaurus 160
Pteranodon 163
Stegosaurus. 165
Space Shuttle 168
Astronaut 170
Recycling 172
Recycling Labels. 174
Lunch Box 175
Snacks 176
Food Pyramid 178
Tooth 180
Toothbrush 181
Toothpaste. 182
Ear 183
Nose 184
Eye 185
Mouth. 186
Hand. 187

Table of Contents *(cont.)*

Math Patterns and Ideas 188

   Analog Clock 189

   Digital Clock 191

   AM/PM Labels 192

   Morning 193

   Noon. 194

   Night 195

   Symbols 196

   Numerals 198

   Domino. 208

   Graph Grid 209

   Pizza Fractions 211

   Apple Fractions. 213

   Pie Fractions. 215

   Candy Bar Fractions 217

   Cash Register 218

   Ruler. 220

   Tape Measure 221

   Measuring Cup 222

   Pints and Quarts 223

   Gallon. 224

Using the Patterns

There are several ways to use the patterns in this book. The pieces are big and easy to cut out and to glue, and they can be used by students as well as by teachers and helpers. Try to laminate pieces you will be placing in your centers for repeated use.

Color–and–Cut Figures and Paper Sculpture

For an easy-to-prepare art project, simply reproduce the patterns on white construction paper, have children color, cut out, and glue pieces together at the tabs so that the finished product looks like the diagram. If the pattern will benefit from moving parts, try using brads instead of glue.

To make a stuffed paper sculpture, trace the outline of the assembled figure onto another blank piece of paper and cut it out. Color or decorate both pieces before assembling. Put the two pieces together and staple around the edges, leaving one side open. Lightly stuff with crumpled newspaper, then staple the opening shut. Add finishing touches and display.

Classroom Decorations and Story Prompts

The patterns can be used on bulletin boards, flannel boards, or magnetic boards. Copy the pattern on heavy stock, assemble, and then laminate. Glue squares of felt or Velcro® to the back for use on the flannel board or attach magnet strips available at craft stores for magnetic board use. You can also hang the patterns from the ceiling with fishing line or use them to create mobiles. Use the shapes and figures to generate classroom discussion about the various themes and to spark ideas for stories and journal writing.

Word Banks

A word bank is a collection of related words that grows as students learn more about the specific topic. Children gain ownership of the word bank as they add more words to the list. You can create a weather word bank with raindrops and clouds or a transportation word bank with cars and trains.

Puppets and Paper Dolls

Give each child a copy of the pattern to color, cut out, and glue to a craft stick for his or her own stick puppet. For a teacher set, use cardstock and laminate before gluing. You may wish to reduce the patterns or use the diagrams of fully assembled figures and enlarge to meet your needs, or make large puppets using a yardstick. Place a set of the laminated, colored patterns without craft sticks in the Drama Area for the students' use. Encourage the children to create their own dramas, and to make new clothes and accessories for the figures.

Big Books and Shape Books

Many of the patterns in this book lend themselves well to big books. Patterns can be used as covers, or they can be decorations for the inside pages. To make a big book, cut two pieces of poster board to the desired size and glue on the colored pattern to one of the pieces. Punch holes down the side and bind with yarn or rings. You can also make a large shape book by running the pattern on cardstock or construction paper, then tracing the shape onto blank cardstock for the back. Trim lined paper to fit inside the covers and bind with yarn, rings, or staples, as is appropriate for the shape of the book. Big books and shape books can be used for class–generated stories, poems, investigations, or reports, or they can be used as individual theme–related journals.

Language Arts Patterns and Ideas

Use the pen, pencil, and eraser as part of your writing center. Display student writing with the pencil or editing rules with the eraser. The eraser can also be used as individual journal covers for editing guidelines and proofreading marks.

The alphabet patterns can be used in a variety of ways. They can serve as a progressive border around the classroom. Every time you introduce a new letter to the students, add the letter to the border. Use the patterns as decorations for your alphabet center, as headings for a bulletin board, or for coloring.

Each letter is decorated with items that begin (or end, in the case of X) with the featured letter. Encourage students to draw other items on separate pages that begin with that letter. Add the drawings, to be bound later into individual alphabet books or for a class big book. Establish a "Letter of the Week" web in the language arts center. Place the featured letter in the center of the web and surround it with pictures and drawings. Real items or magazine cutouts can also be glued into the letter books or included in the web.

Use the alphabet letters as covers for file folder activities in the language arts center or create individual files to add pictures for the different letters as students come across them. When it is time to do your webs, you will be ready.

The letters can also be reduced to create flash cards or alphabet cards to be used for creating words in the alphabet center. Make two sets of cards and use them for a memory game. Make lots of letters, cover them with contact paper, and place them in a basket in the center. See how long it takes before students start using them to spell their names and the new words they are learning. Give each student in the class a letter at circle time and see if they can arrange themselves in alphabetical order.

Use the nursery rhyme patterns to introduce a unit on Mother Goose. The patterns can be used on the flannel board to retell the rhymes or make stick puppets and place them in the language arts center. Create a puppet theater for your students and give them opportunities to present the rhymes to each other. Have stick puppets for all the rhymes and see if students can sort them out. What other stories could the puppets tell? What might the three little kittens mother tell Humpty Dumpty about sitting on a wall?

You can also use the patterns to create stuffed paper sculptures as an art project during the unit. Turn one bulletin board into Mother Goose Land and have the children help place each piece in the appropriate area. Try a green background with blue sky and some fluffy clouds.

Little Miss Muffet could be used to introduce a unit on spiders, while Humpty Dumpty could become part of an egg study or a unit on safety. Use the Hickory, Dickory Dock clock to mark special times in your classroom.

The Three Little Kittens can join the Black Sheep with his three bags of wool to create interesting math questions and stories. If each kitten had two mittens, how many mittens were there altogether? If each child in the class colors and cuts out three bags of wool, how many bags of wool will the whole class have? Count by threes to find out!

Make up new rhymes for Hickory Dickory Dock to correspond with 2:00 through 12:00. Record the new verses in a class big book in a clock shape. The patterns for this rhyme can also be used in the math center to explore the concept of time.

Fountain Pen

Attach pen cap to the tab.

Tab

Pencil

Join the pencil in the middle at the tab.

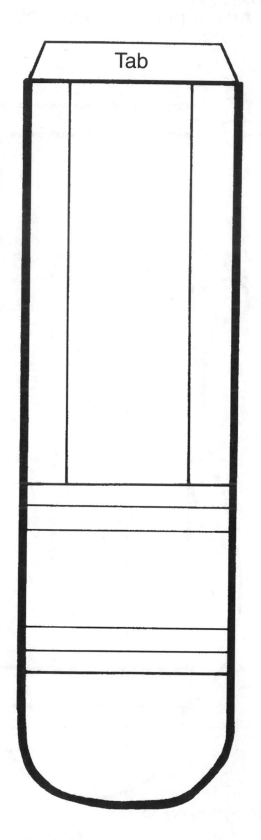

Tab

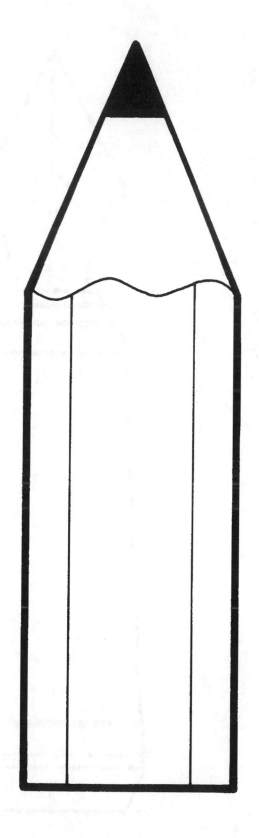

Eraser

Alphabet—A

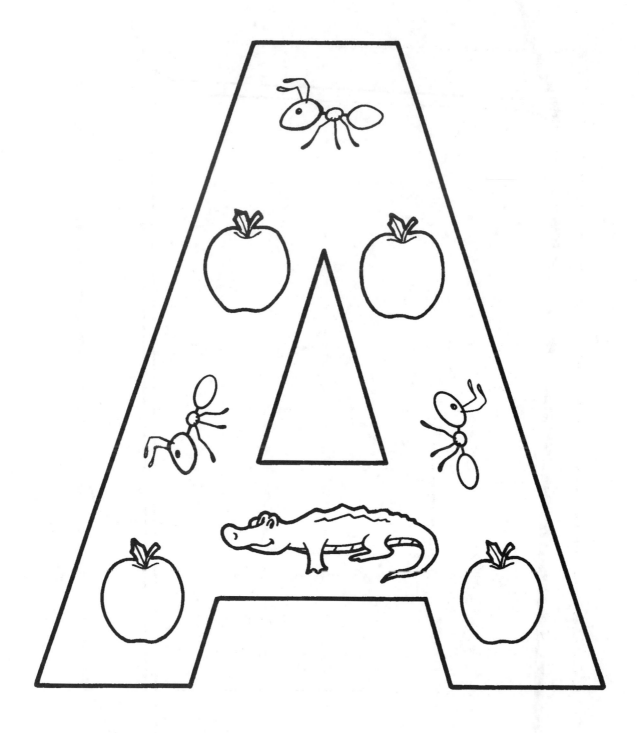

10

Alphabet—B

Alphabet—c

Alphabet—D

Alphabet—E

Alphabet-F

Alphabet—G

16

Alphabet—H

Alphabet—I

Alphabet—J

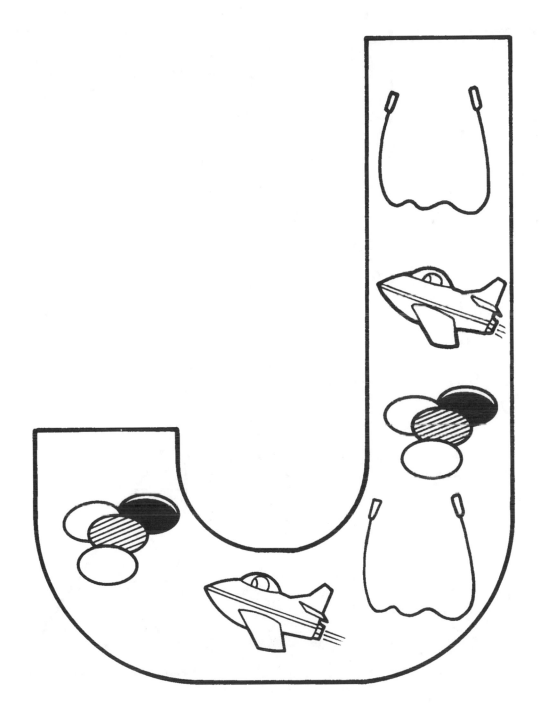

Alphabet—K

Alphabet—L

Alphabet—M

Alphabet—N

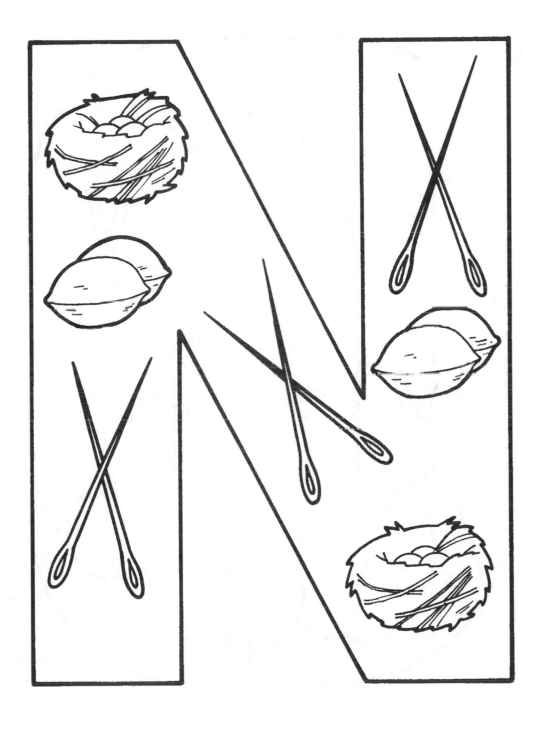

Alphabet—O

Alphabet—P

Alphabet—Q

Alphabet–R

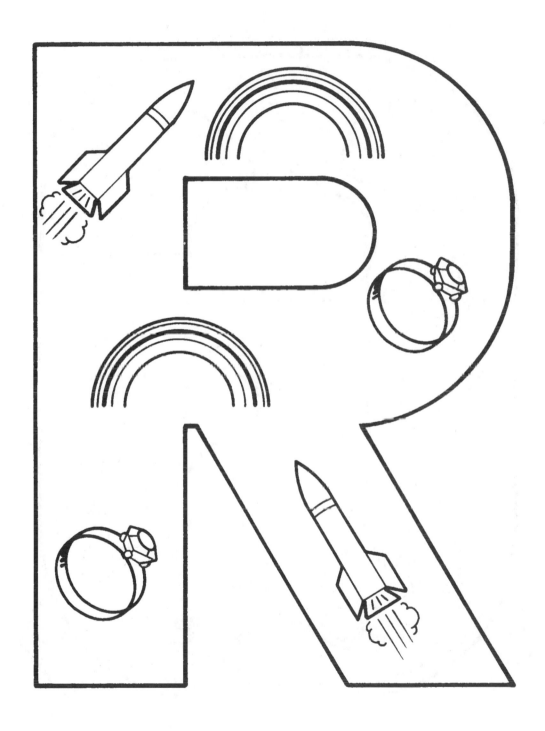

Alphabet—S

Alphabet—T

Alphabet—U

30

Alphabet—V

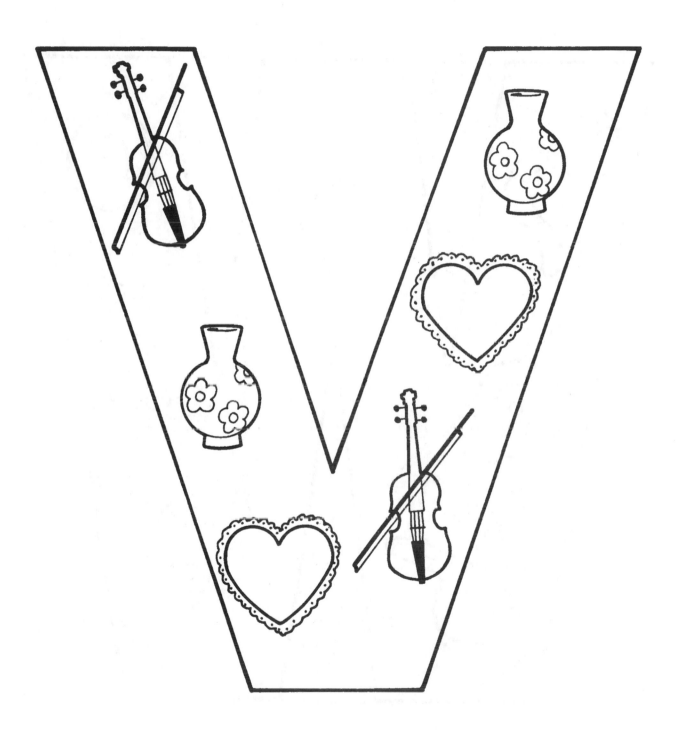

Alphabet—W

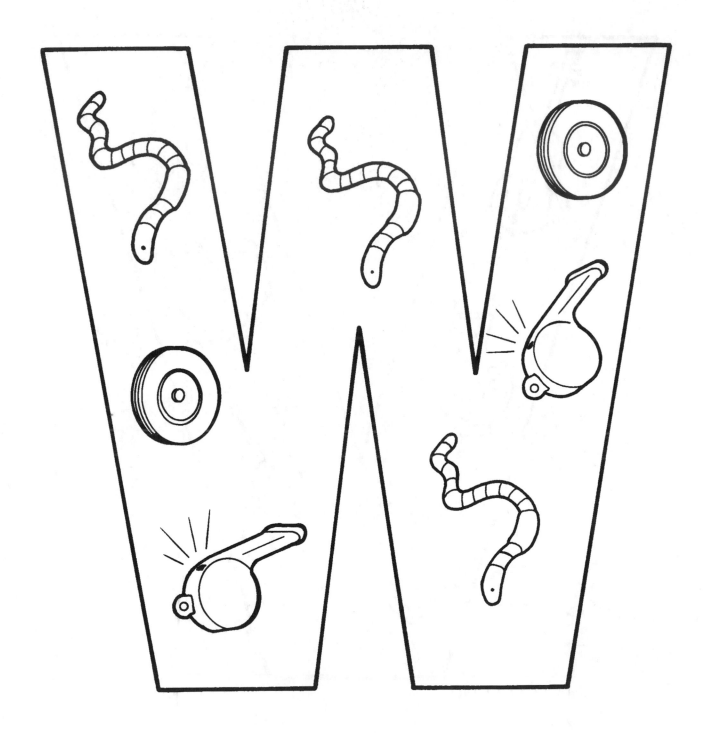

Alphabet–X

Alphabet—Y

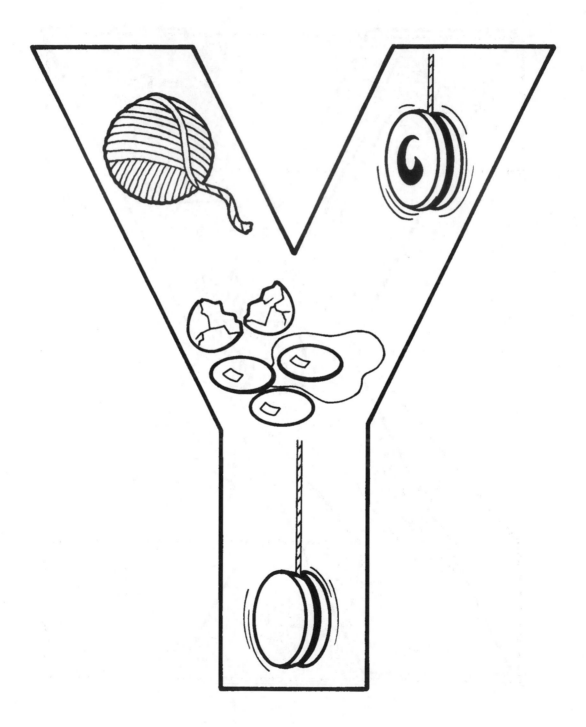

Alphabet—Z

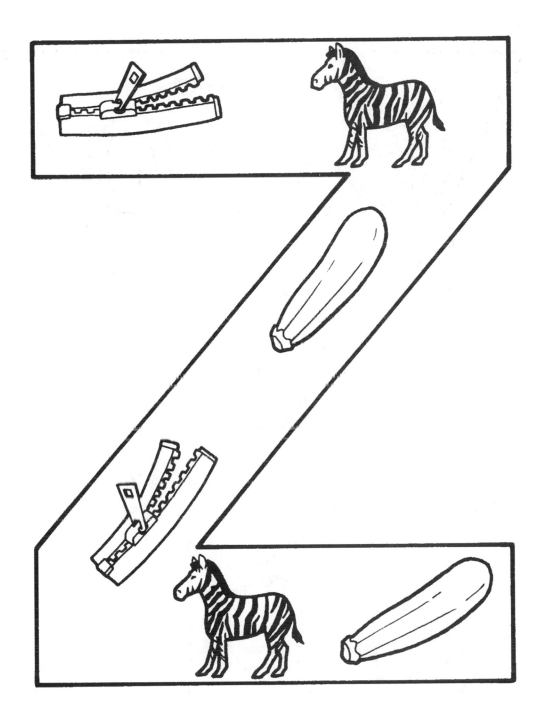

Little Miss Muffet

Use pages 37–38. Connect Miss Muffet at the tab. Cut out the spider and bowl and arrange as desired.

Tab

Little Miss Muffet *(cont.)*

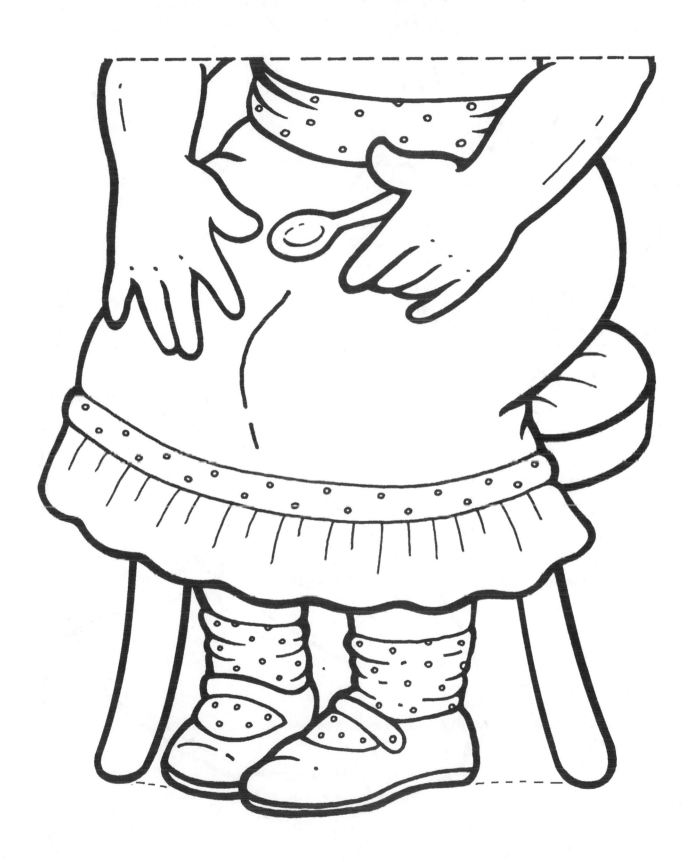

Little Miss Muffet *(cont.)*

Humpty Dumpty

Use pages 39–41.

Humpty Dumpty *(cont.)*

40

Humpty Dumpty (cont.)

The Three Little Kittens

Use pages 42–44.

The Three Little Kittens *(cont.)*

Mother

The Three Little Kittens *(cont.)*

44

Jack Jumped Over a Candlestick

Baa, Baa, Black Sheep

Use pages 46–48. Connect the sheep at the tab and color black. Use with the bag of wool on page 48.

Tab

Baa, Baa, Black Sheep (cont.)

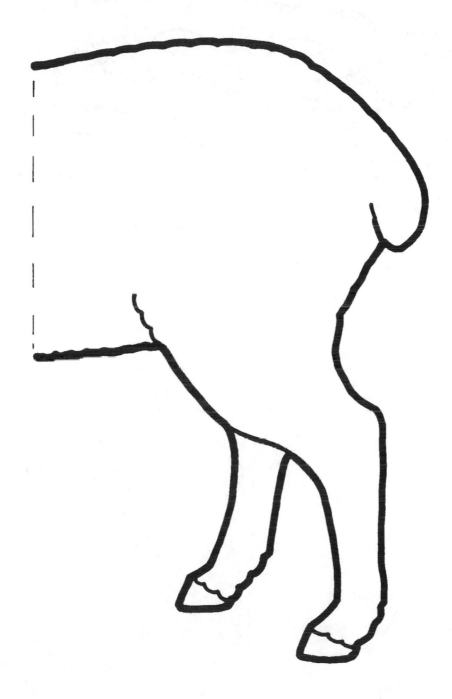

Baa, Baa, Black Sheep *(cont.)*

Make three bags and color the wool black. The bags may be any color.

Hickory Dickory Dock

Use pages 49–51. Connect the clock at the tab. Attach the hands and the mouse from page 51.

Hickory Dickory Dock *(cont.)*

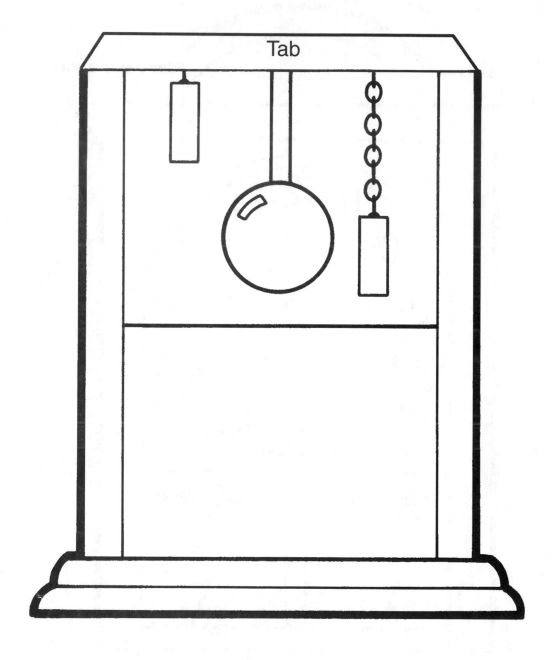

Tab

Hickory Dickory Dock *(cont.)*

Use a brad to attach the hands to the clock.

Social Studies Patterns and Ideas

Use the White House and Capitol patterns to introduce important American buildings to your students. Have students create their own patterns of their homes and display them on the bulletin board with the White House. Include a Venn diagram of My House and the President's House.

The Statue of Liberty makes a great bulletin board display or a fun art project. Have students color, cut out, and assemble Lady Liberty (be sure to discuss why she has a greenish hue), then trace onto a piece of butcher paper. Cut out the second figure and staple to the first, leaving one side open to stuff with crumpled newspaper, then staple the opening closed.

Display student-assembled eagles by suspending them from the ceiling with fishing line. Gather students' thoughts on liberty and what it means to be free and record on the bulletin board around the Liberty Bell or in a Liberty Bell Big Book.

The various community helper patterns can be used as part of a unit on occupations or on helpers in our community. Emphasize that both men and women can hold any one of these positions. Use the figures as puppets, flannel board figures, story prompts, or art projects. Each figure can also be used as part of his or her own unit; for example, the fire fighter can be used as part of a fire safety unit or the dentist can be used with the tooth and toothbrush for a unit on dental hygiene. Have students add to the patterns given with pictures from magazines and create a wall entitled, "What I Want to be When I Grow Up." Add student names beneath their chosen goals.

A variety of transportation vehicles are included. Graph how many students have been in a plane, a train, or a truck. Chart how students arrive at school. Create stories using the cars, trucks and trains or make a Transportation Big Book.

Use the patterns of children from other cultures in their traditional dress to introduce a unit on Children from Other Lands. Place the figures on the bulletin board around a map of the world. The pattern of the boy in play clothes might be used to represent North America or students anywhere in everyday attire. Compare everyday clothes with those worn on special occasions. These patterns can serve to open the door for further study. Have students research their own heritage and create a figure to add to the bulletin board.

The patterns of the cowboy, horse and steer, pioneers and covered wagons can be used to introduce an important part of the American past. Students can create their own brands to "decorate" their steers. Chart reasons for moving west. Lists of what supplies were needed can be recorded on the covered wagon. Creat an entire wagon train on the bulletin board or around the classroom. Have students add family members to reflect their own families.

The Native Americans depicted in the patterns are from the Iroquois tribe of the northeastern United States. Use them to introduce a unit on Native American cultures. Students can investigate different types of Native American shelters by creating the three–dimensional projects included. Encourage students to find out more about other types of homes and shelters. Explore why certain Native American groups used wood and others used hides to build their homes. Compare homes of long ago with current building styles.

White House

Use pages 53–54. Cut out and connect at the tab.

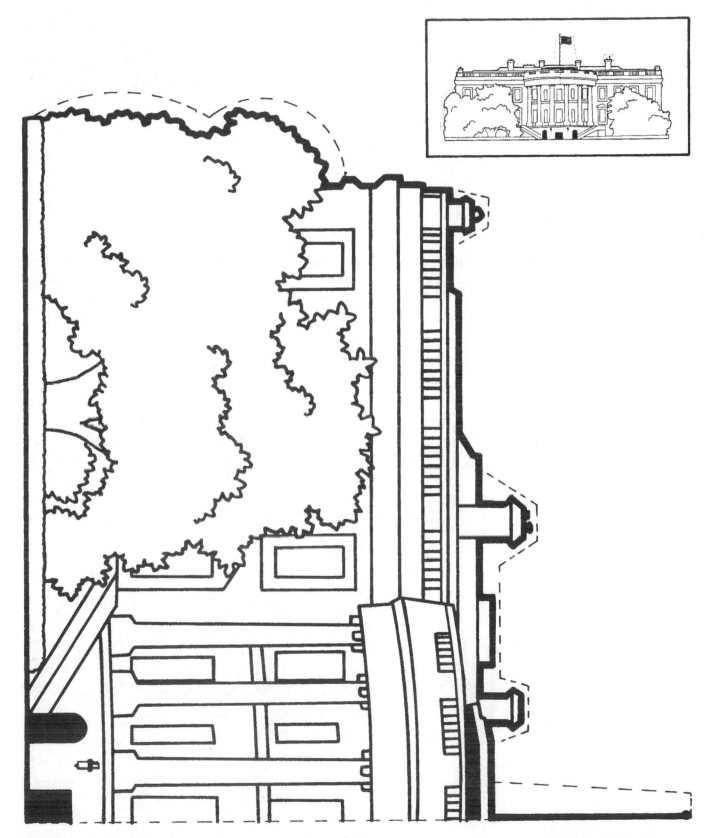

White House *(cont.)*

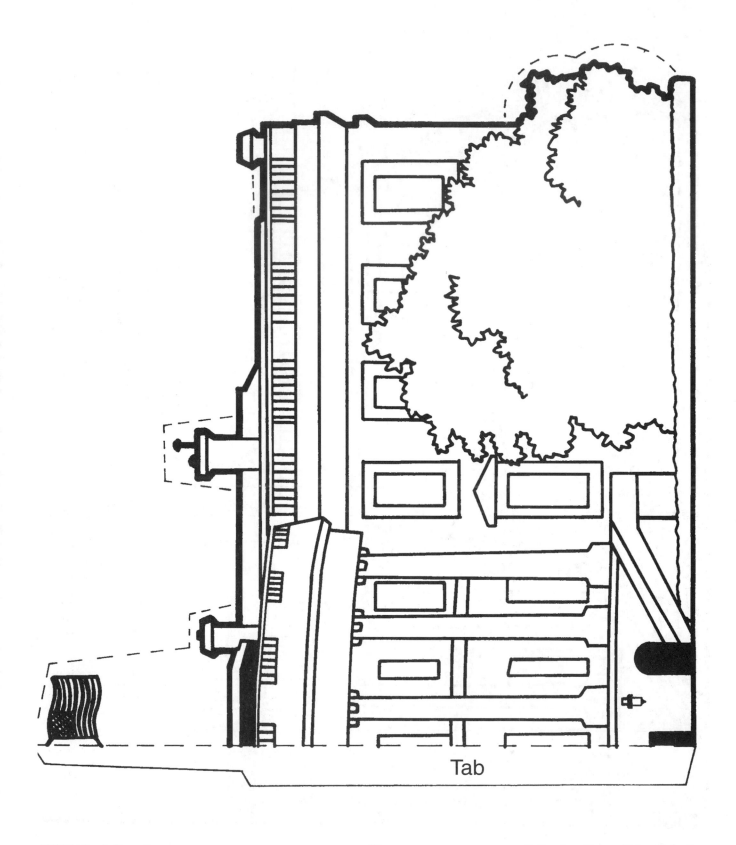

Tab

Capitol

Use pages 55–56. Cut out and connect at the tab.

Capitol *(cont.)*

Tab

Eagle

Use pages 57–58. Attach wings behind the eagle at the tabs.

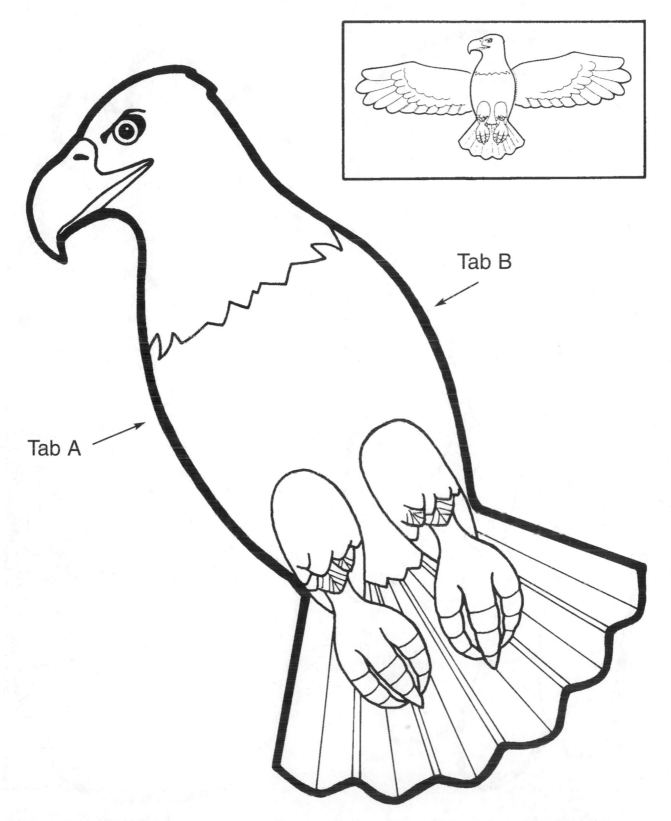

Tab B

Tab A

Eagle *(cont.)*

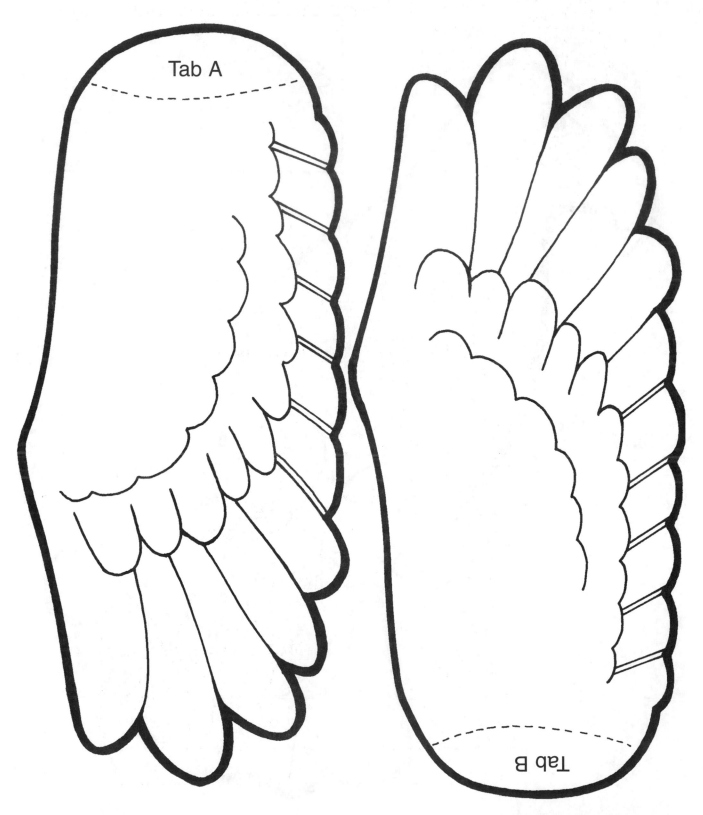

Statue of Liberty

Use pages 59–61. Cut out the three sections of the Statue of Liberty. Attach torso at Tab A. Connect pedestal at Tab B. Color and display statue.

Tab A

Statue of Liberty *(cont.)*

Statue of Liberty *(cont.)*

Tab B

Liberty Bell

Use pages 62–63. Cut out and connect at the tab.

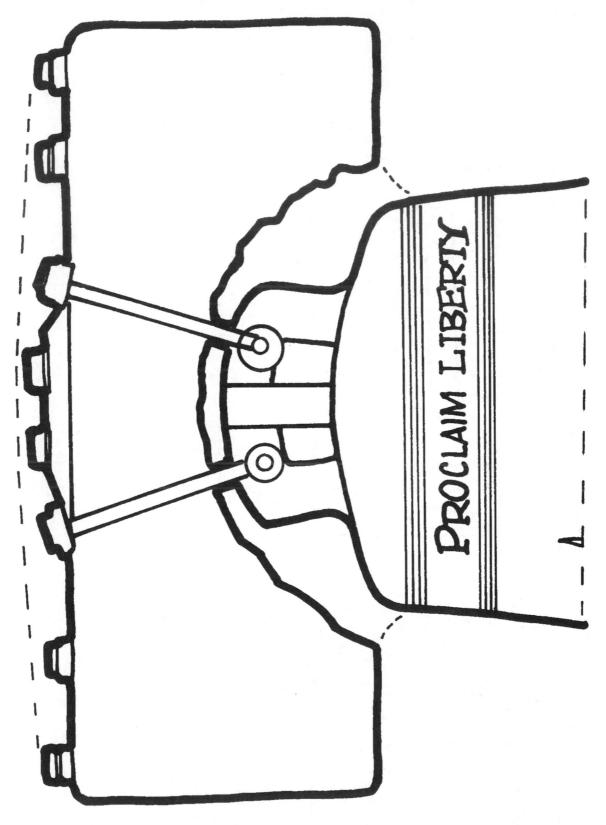

Liberty Bell *(cont.)*

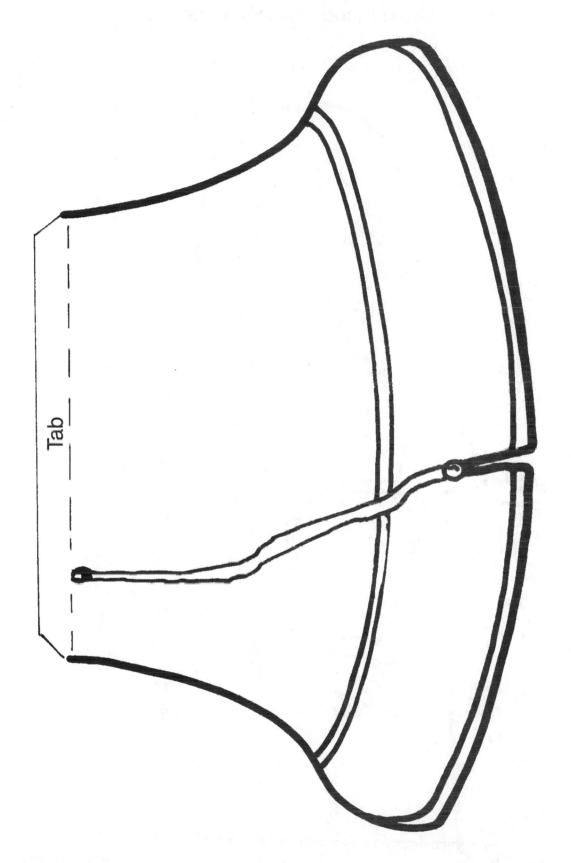

Tab

Doctor

Use pages 64-65. Cut out and connect at the tab.

Doctor *(cont.)*

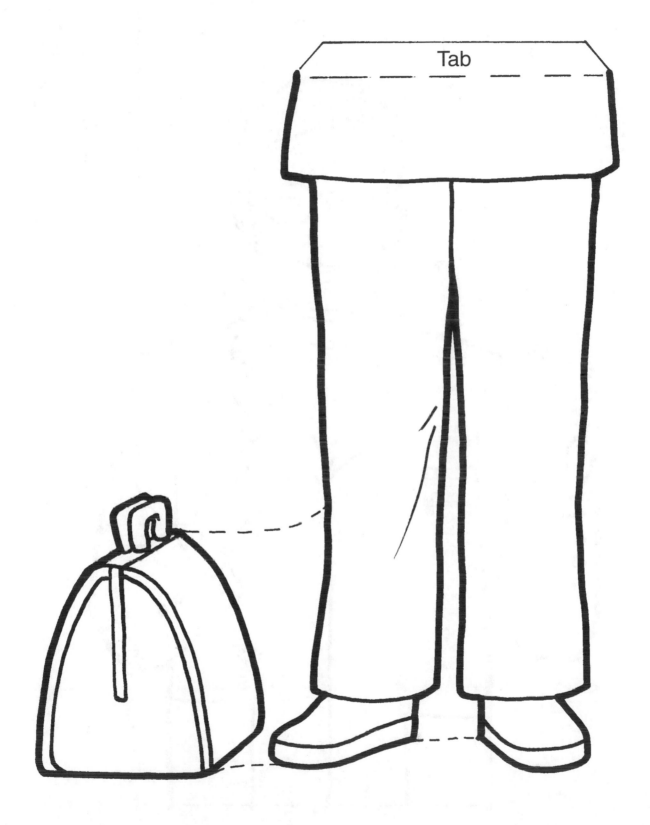

Tab

Dentist

Use pages 66–67. Cut out and connect at the tab.

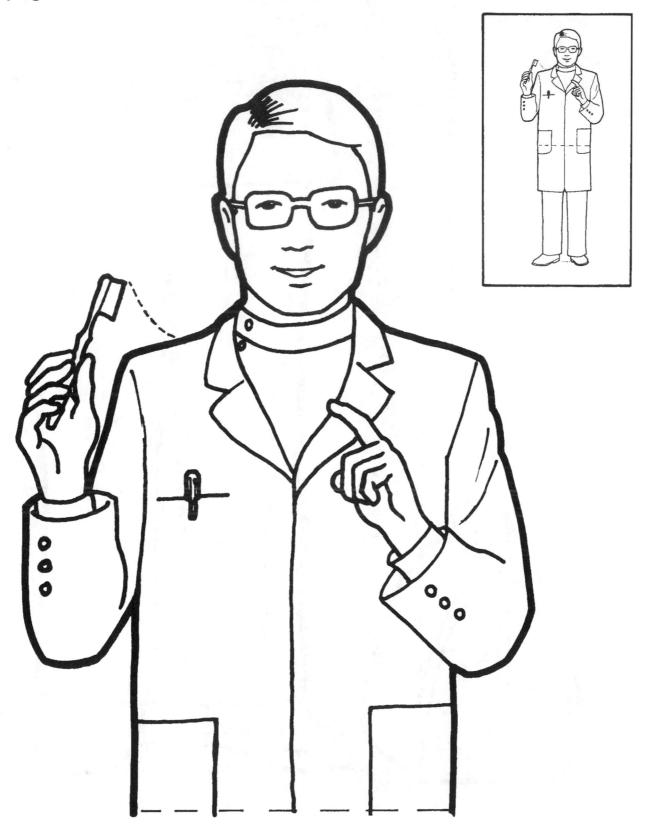

Dentist (cont.)

Tab

Mail Carrier

Use pages 68–69. Cut out mail carrier and connect at Tab A. Attach mailbag at Tab B (behind elbow).

Tab A

Mail Carrier *(cont.)*

Tab B

Police Officer

Use pages 70–71. Cut out and connect at the tab.

Police Officer *(cont.)*

Tab

Firefighter

Use pages 72–74.

Cut out the firefighter and connect at the tab.
Use hydrant on page 74.

Tab

Firefighter *(cont.)*

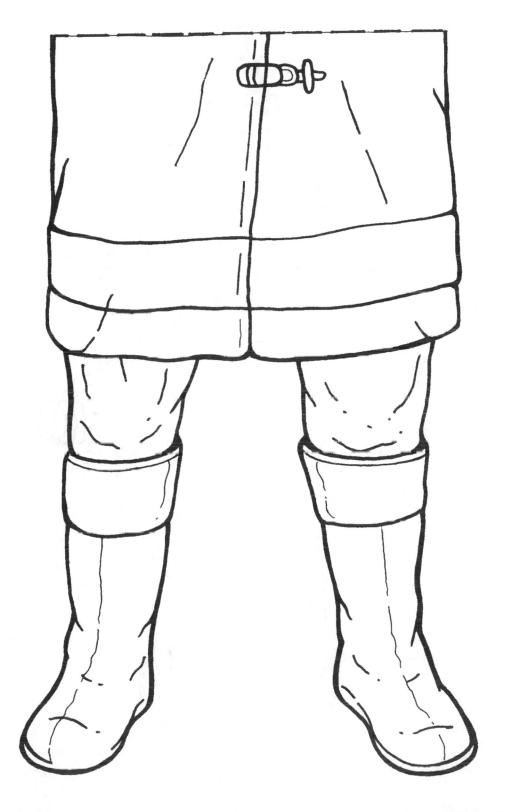

Fire Hydrant

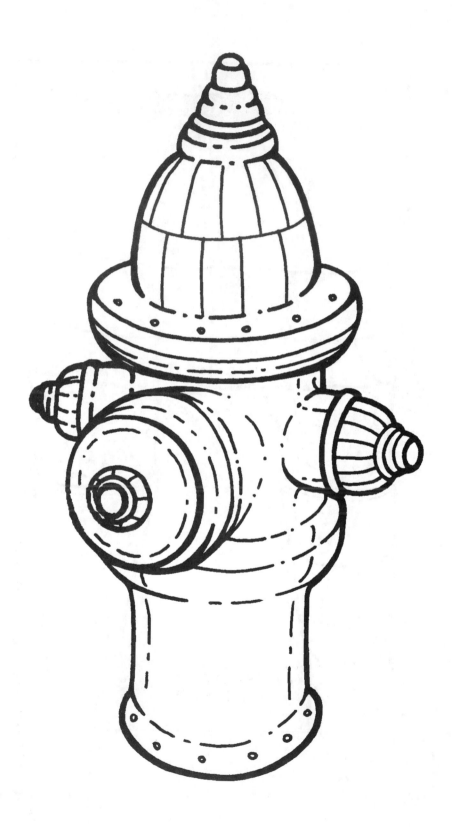

Teacher

Use pages 75–76. Cut out the teacher and connect at the tab.

Teacher *(cont.)*

Tab

Car

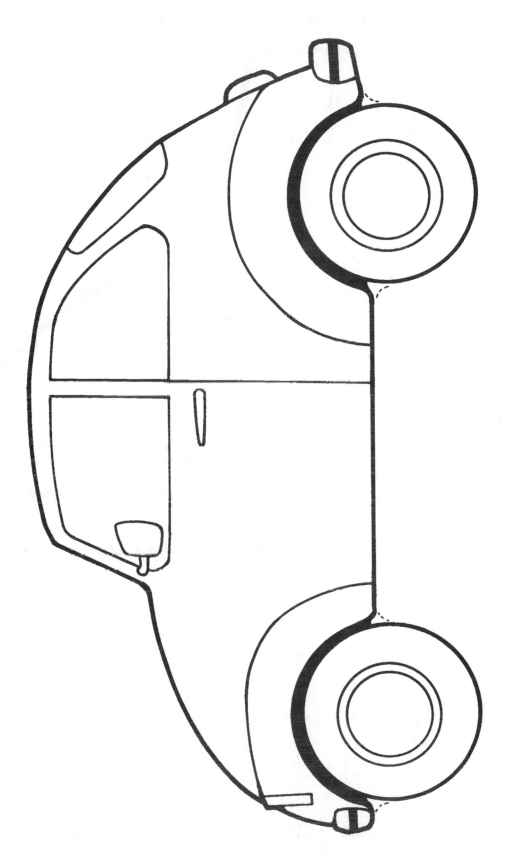

Truck

Use pages 78–79. Cut out and connect at the tab.

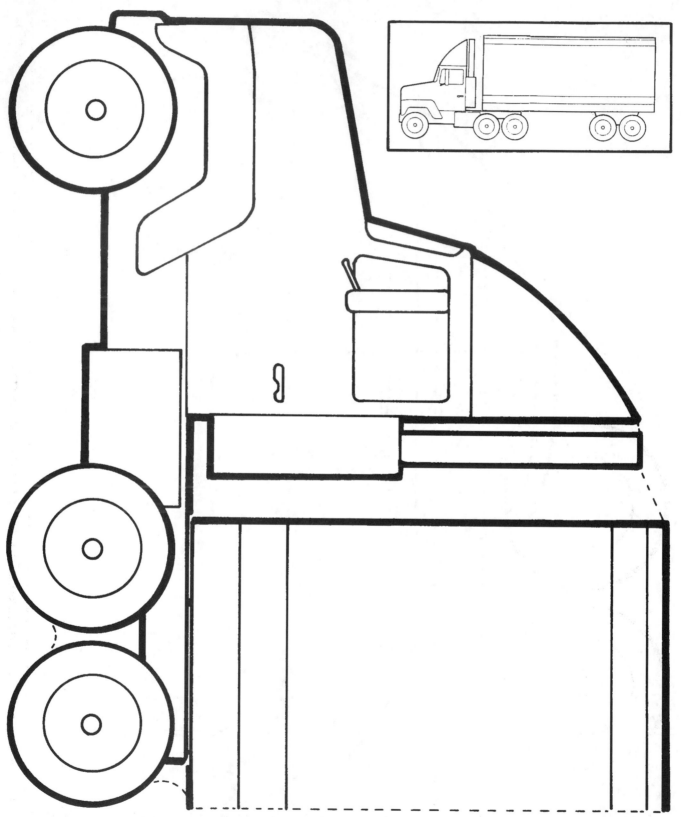

Truck *(cont.)*

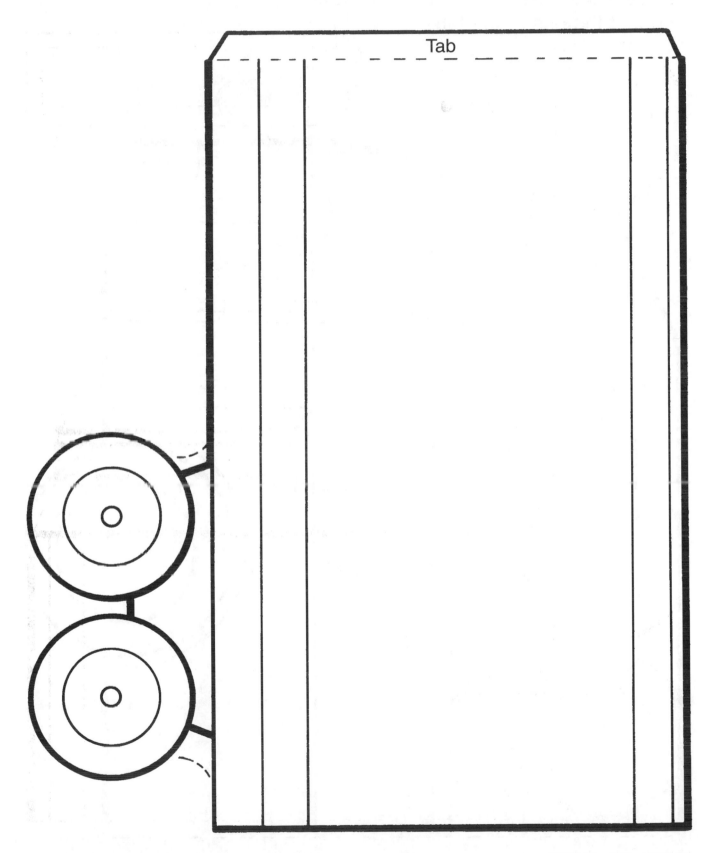

Tab

Bus

Use pages 80–81.
Connect the bus at the tab.

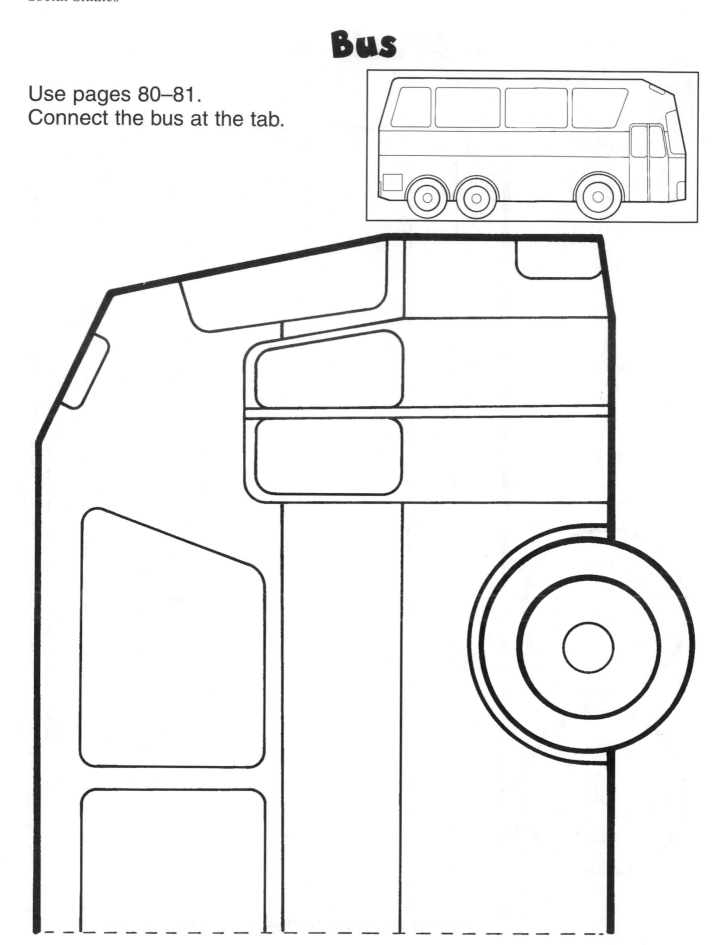

80

Bus (cont.)

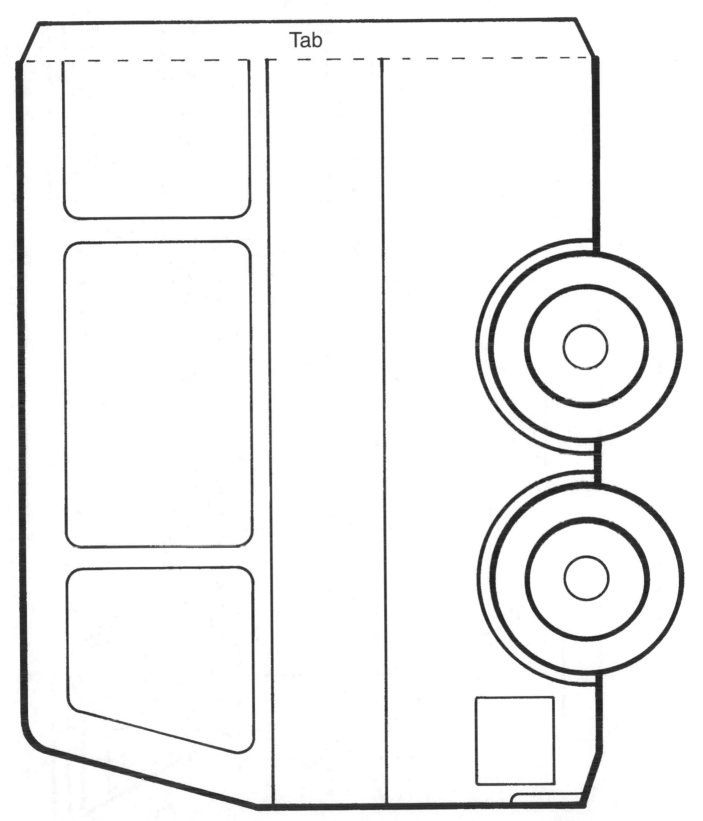

Tab

Train

Use pages 82–84. Connect the engine to the boxcar at Tab A.
Connect the caboose to the boxcar at Tab B.

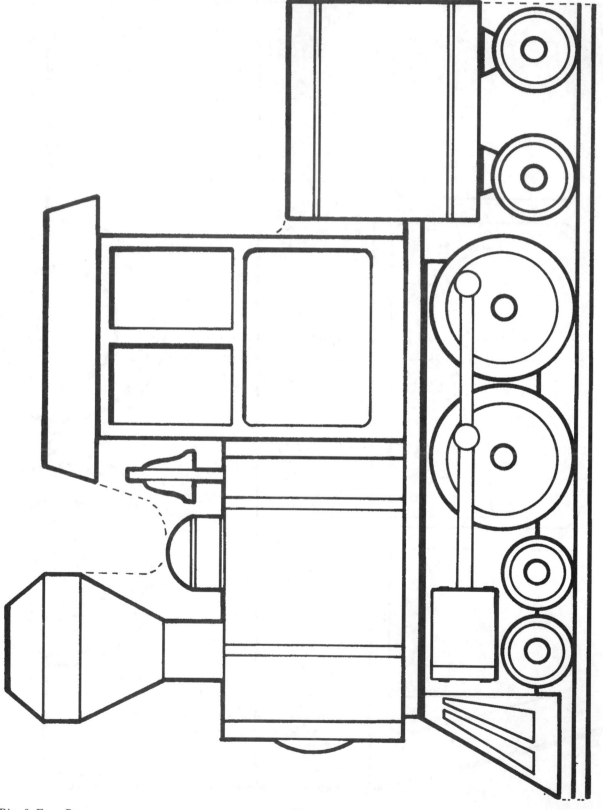

Train *(cont.)*

Tab A

Train *(cont.)*

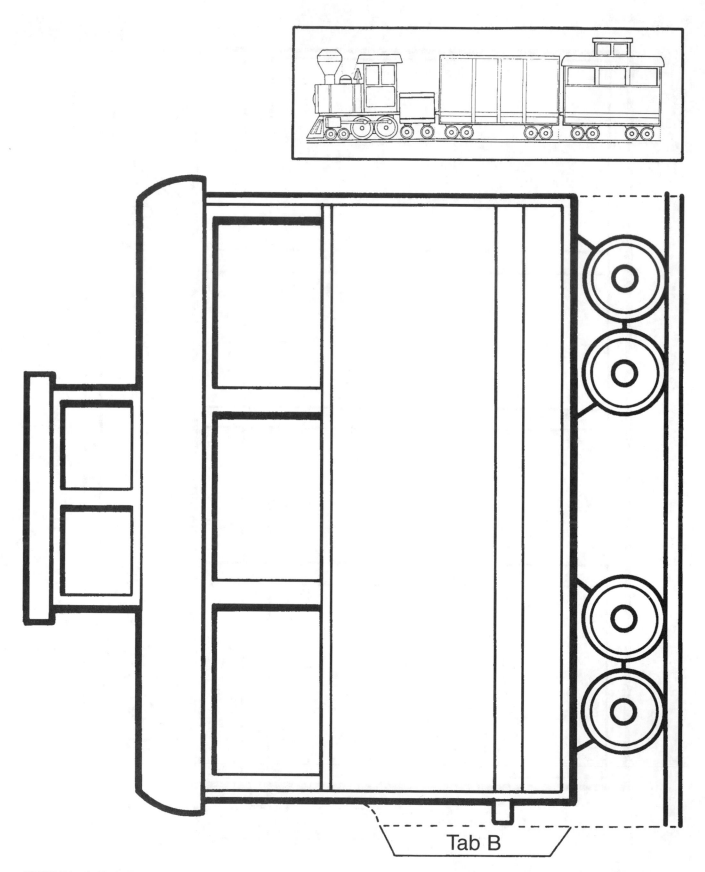

Tab B

Airplane

Use pages 85–86. See diagram for wing placement.

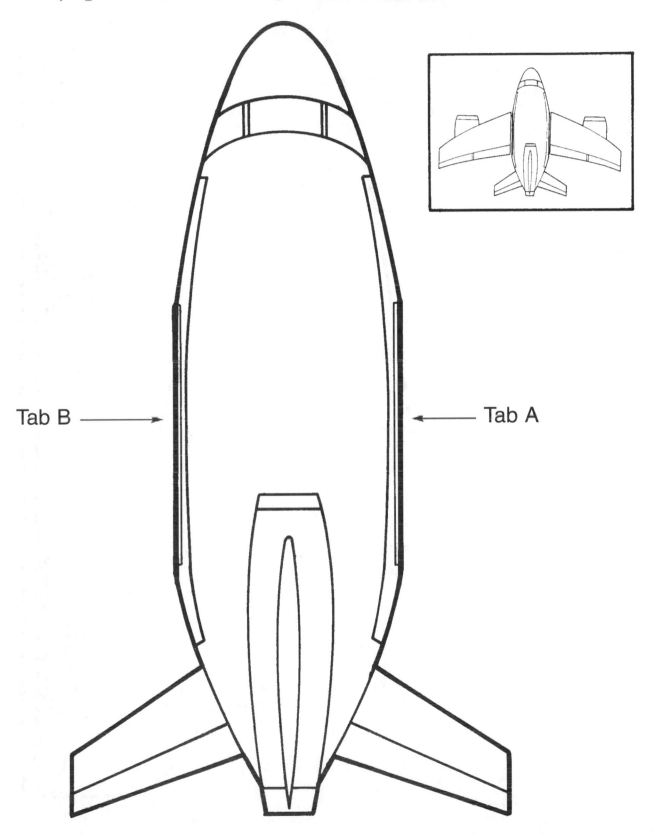

Tab B ←

Tab A →

Airplane *(cont.)*

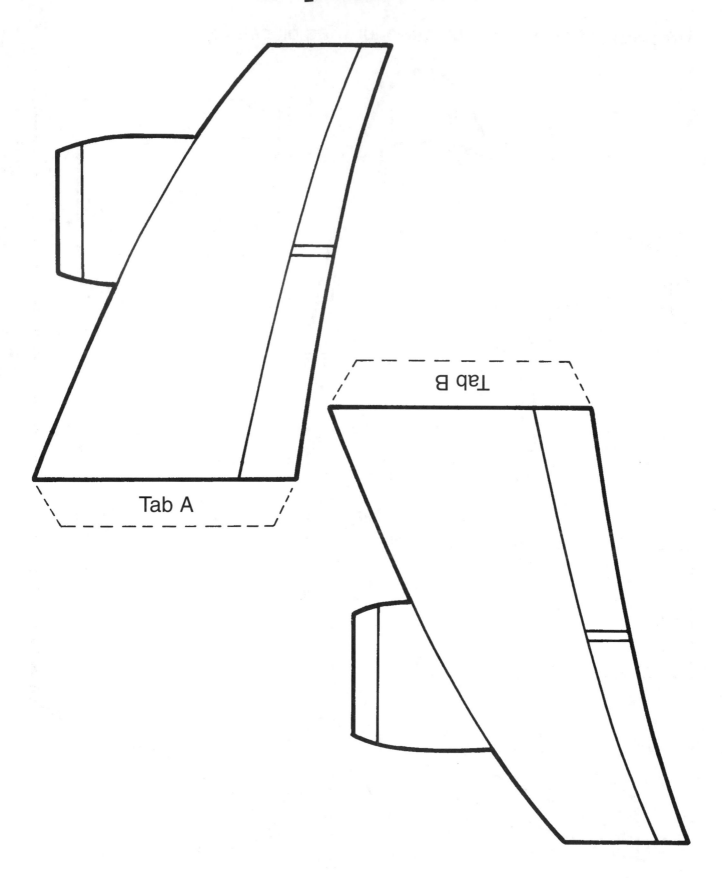

Tab A

Tab B

Cruise Ship

Use pages 87–88. Connect the cruise ship at the tab.

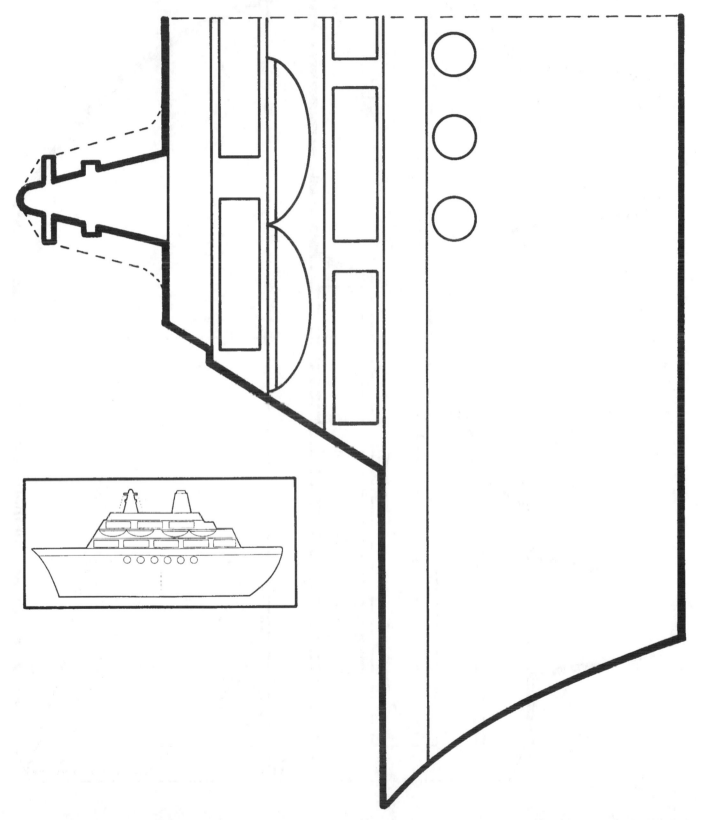

Cruise Ship (cont.)

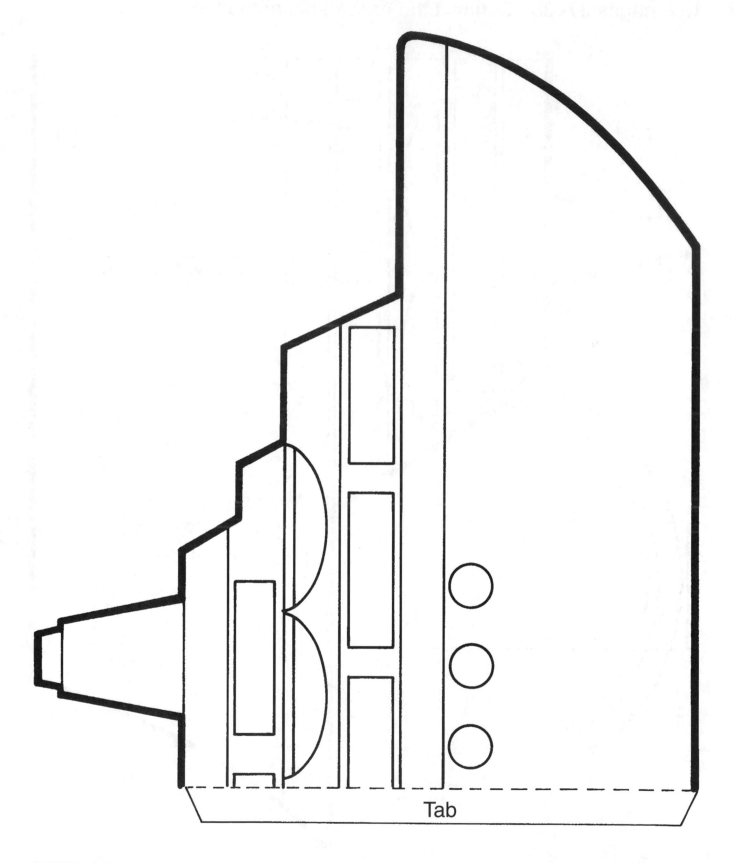

Tab

Bicycle

Use pages 89–90. Connect the bike at the tab.

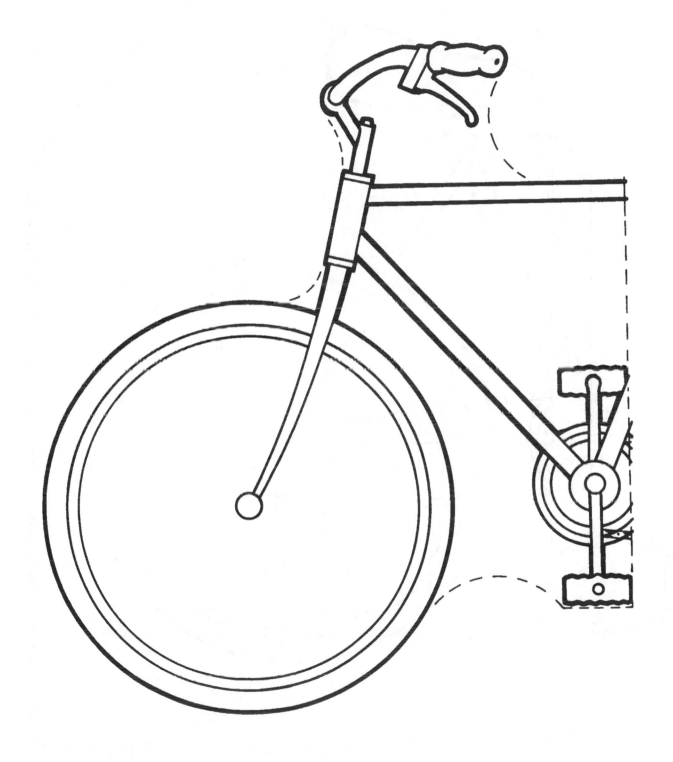

Bicycle *(cont.)*

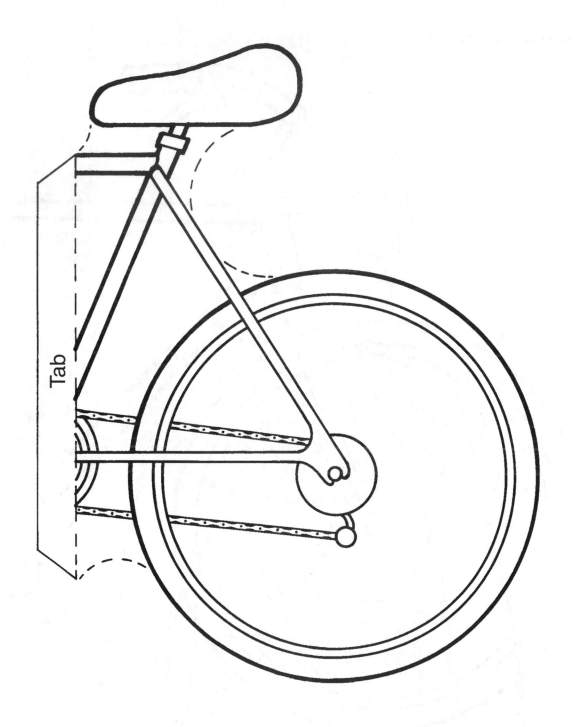

Tab

Clothing and Costumes of the World

Tanzania

Use pages 91–92. Cut out and connect at the tab.

Clothing and Costumes
of the World *(cont.)*

Tanzania

Tab

Clothing and Costumes
of the World *(cont.)*

Japan

Use pages 93–94.

Cut out and connect
at the tab.

Clothing and Costumes of the World *(cont.)*

Japan

Tab

94

Clothing and Costumes
of the World *(cont.)*

Argentina

Use pages 95–96. Cut out and connect at the tab.

Clothing and Costumes of the World *(cont.)*

Argentina

Tab

Clothing and Costumes of the World *(cont.)*

Holland

Use pages 97–98. Cut out and connect at the tab.

Clothing and Costumes
of the World *(cont.)*

Holland

Tab

Clothing and Costumes
of the World *(cont.)*

Australia

Use pages 99–100. Cut out and connect at the tab.

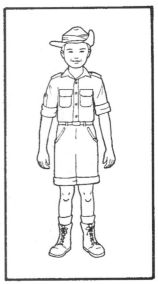

Clothing and Costumes of the World *(cont.)*

Australia

Tab

Clothing and Costumes
of the World (cont.)

Play Clothes

Use pages 101–102. Cut out and connect at the tab.

Play Clothes *(cont.)*

Tab

Cowboy

Use pages 103–105. Cut out and connect at the tab. Add the hat and the lasso from page 105.

Cowboy *(cont.)*

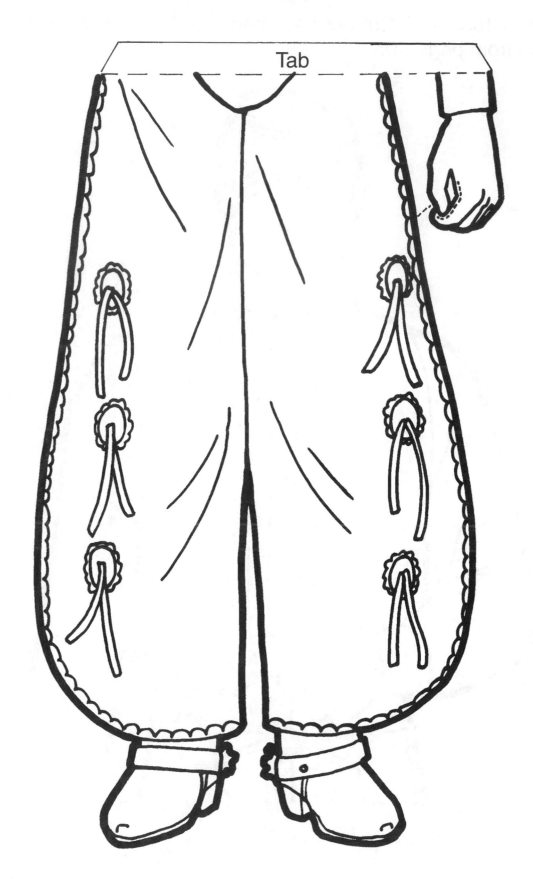

Tab

Cowboy (cont.)

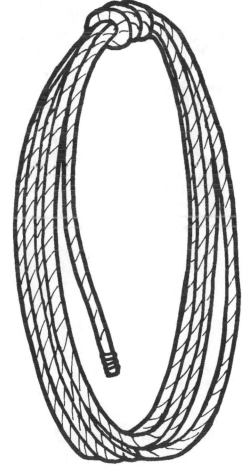

Longhorn Steer

Use pages 106–107. Connect the steer at the tab.

Longhorn Steer (cont.)

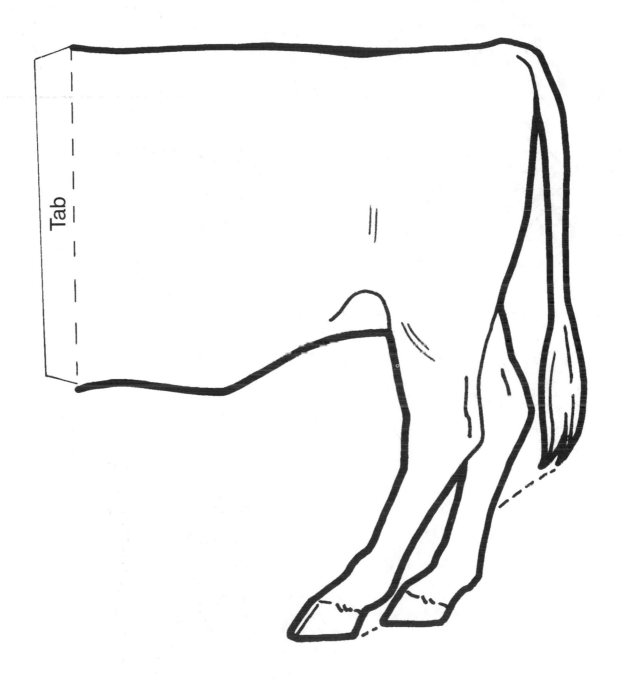

Horse

Use pages 108–109. Connect the horse at the tab.

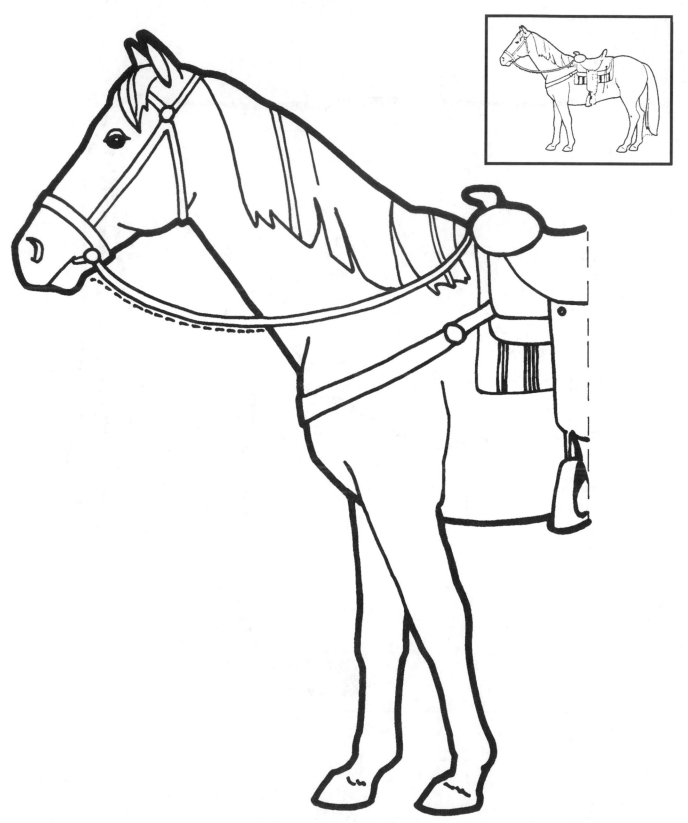

Horse *(cont.)*

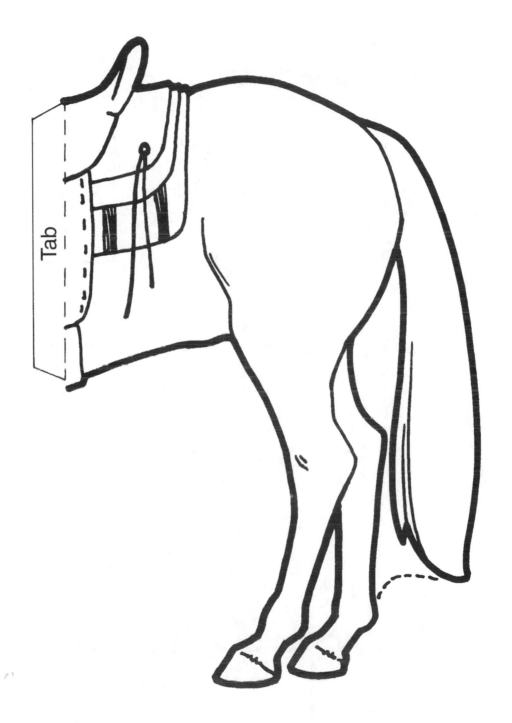

Tab

Pioneer Boy

Use pages 110–111. Connect the boy at the tab.

Pioneer Boy *(cont.)*

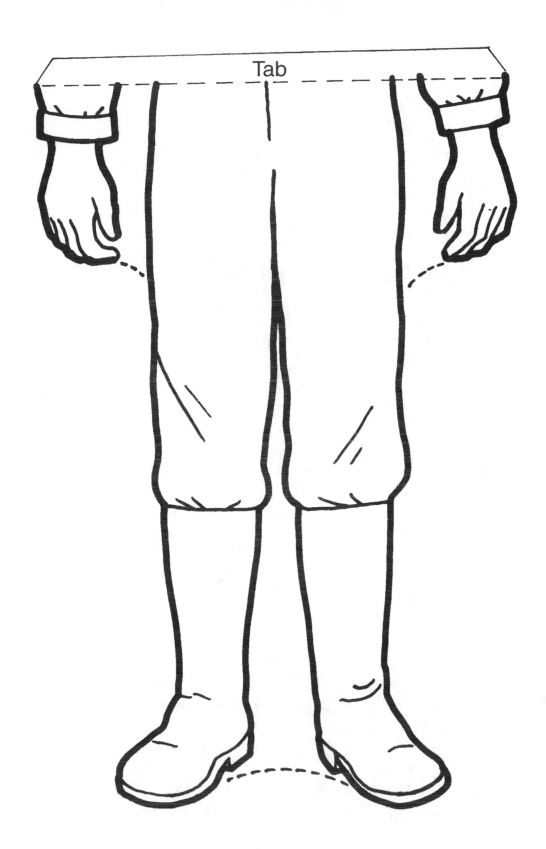

Tab

Pioneer Girl

Use pages 112–113. Connect the girl at the tab.

Pioneer Girl (cont.)

Tab

Covered Wagon

Use pages 114–117.
See directions on page 115.

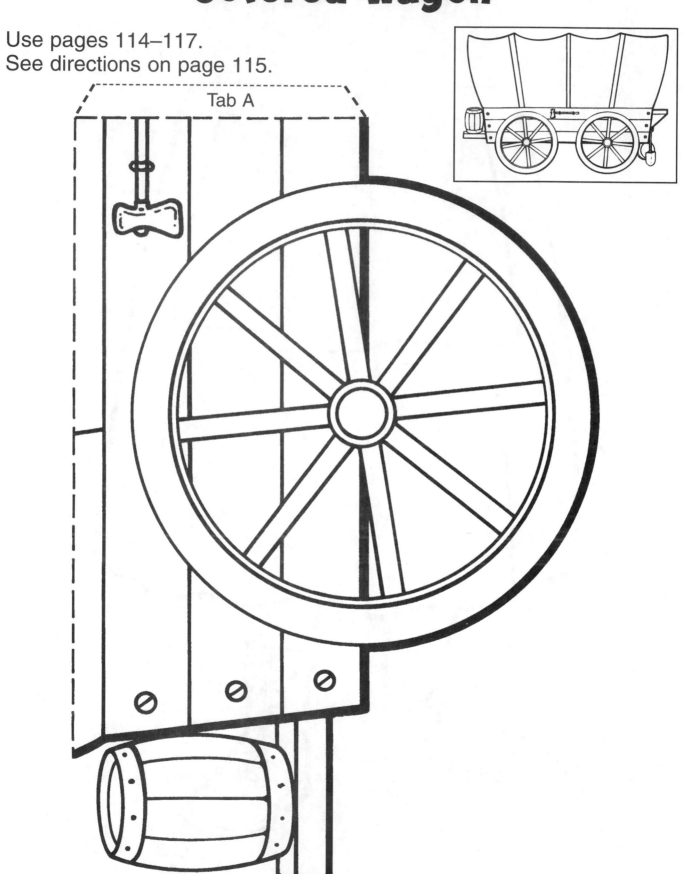

Tab A

114

Covered Wagon *(cont.)*

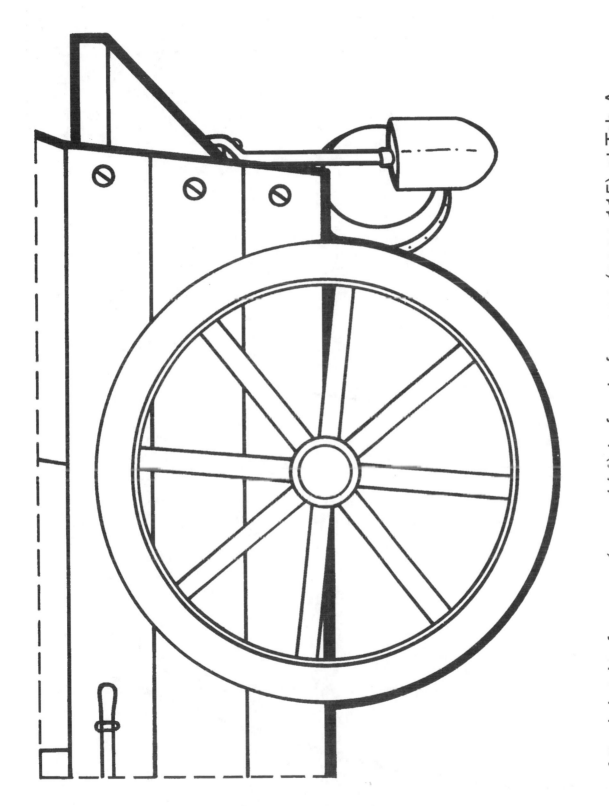

Attach back of wagon (page 114) to front of wagon (page 115) at Tab A. Connect wagon covers at Tab C. Attach completed wagon to wagon covers (pages 116–117) at Tabs B. See page 114 for completed wagon diagram.

Covered Wagon *(cont.)*

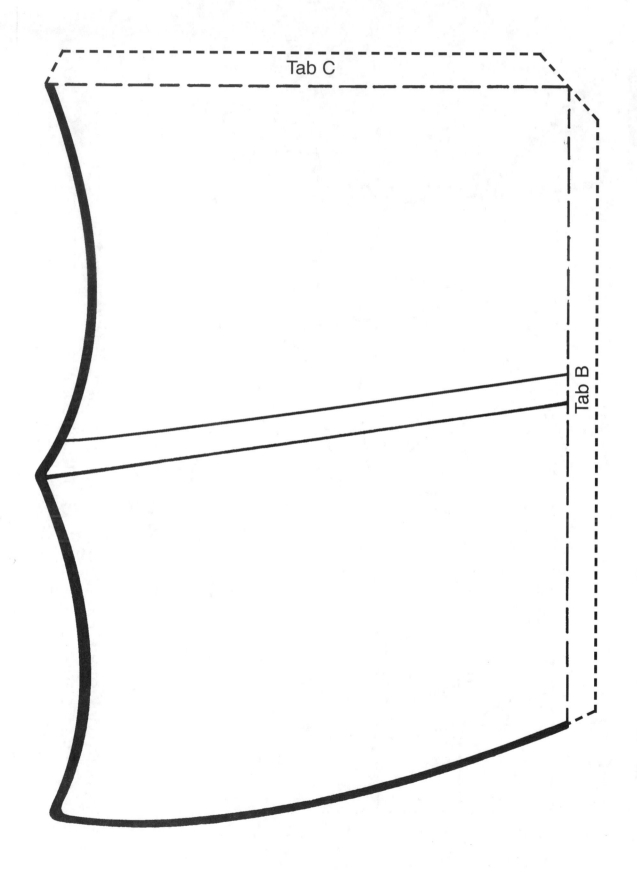

Covered Wagon *(cont.)*

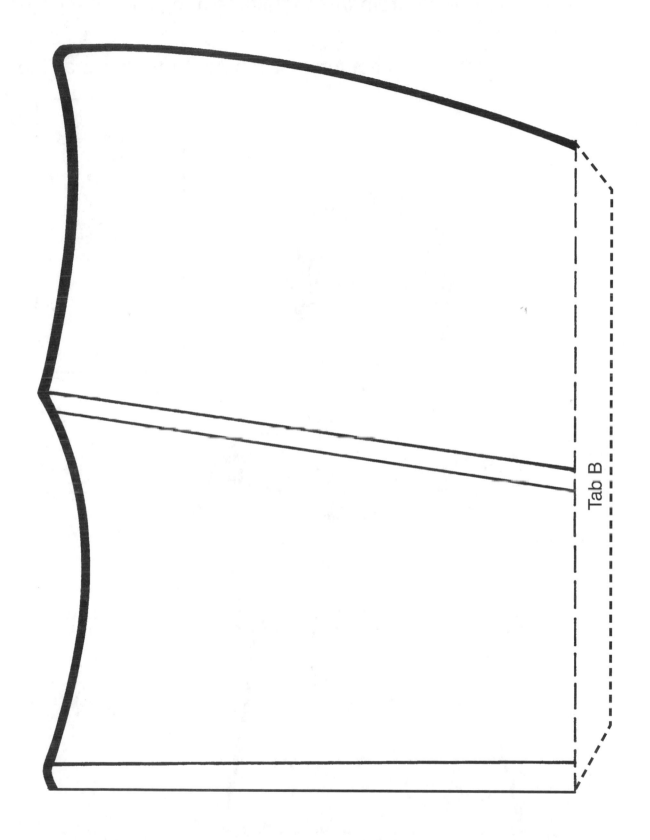

Tab B

Iroquois Female and Infant

The Iroquois people are from the northeastern region of the United States.

Use pages 118-120. Connect torso at Tab A. Attach arms at Tabs B and C.

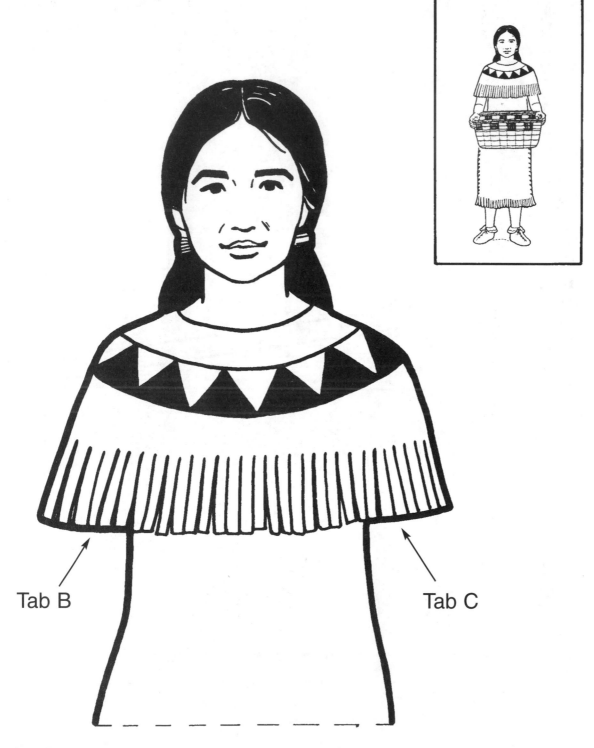

Tab B

Tab C

Iroquois Female and Infant *(cont.)*

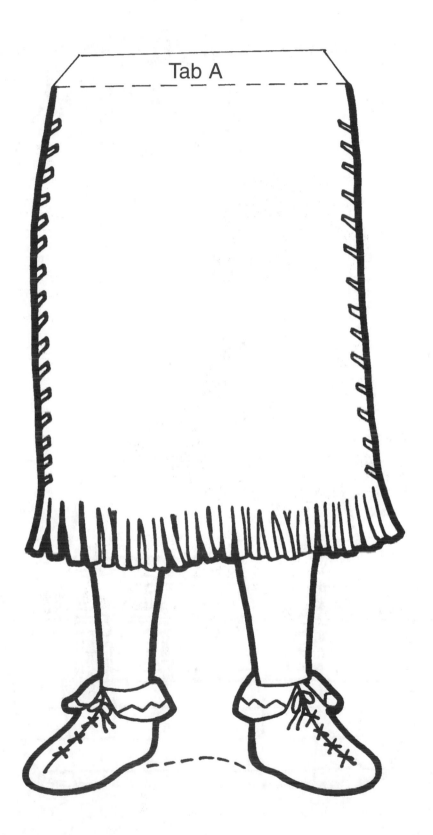

Tab A

Iroquois Female and Infant (cont.)

Baby in a
Cradle Board

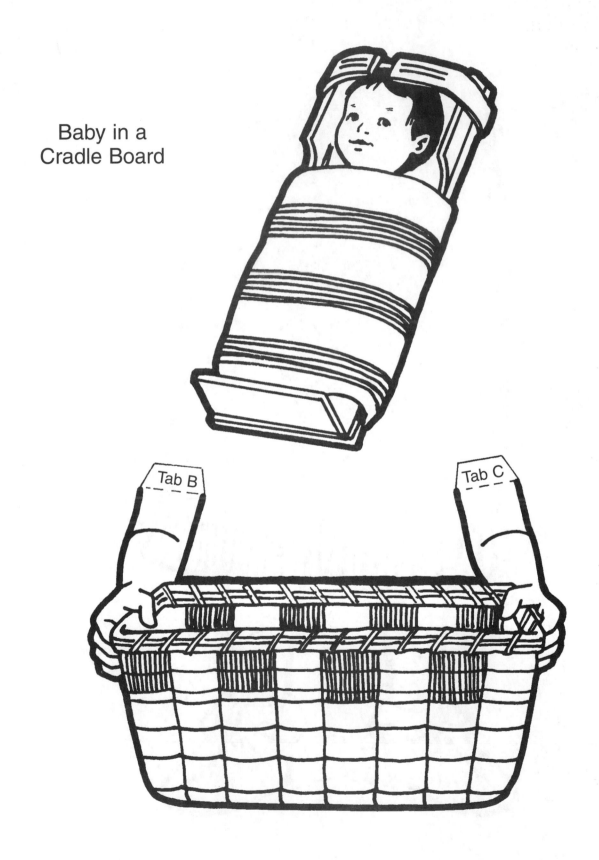

Tab B

Tab C

Iroquois Male

Use pages 121–123. Connect torso at Tab A.
Attach arms at Tabs B and C.

Tab B

Tab C

Iroquois Male *(cont.)*

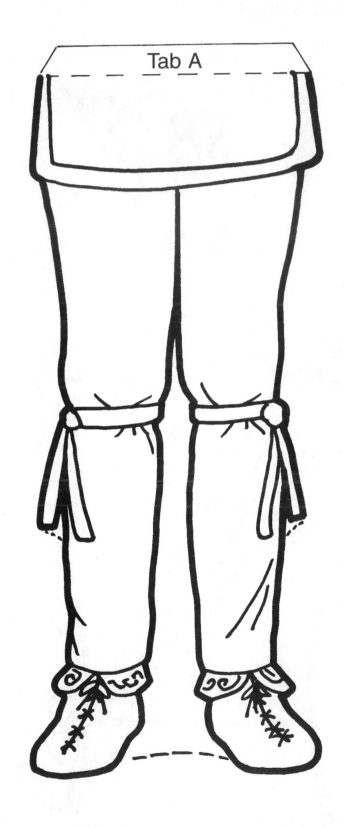

Iroquois Male (cont.)

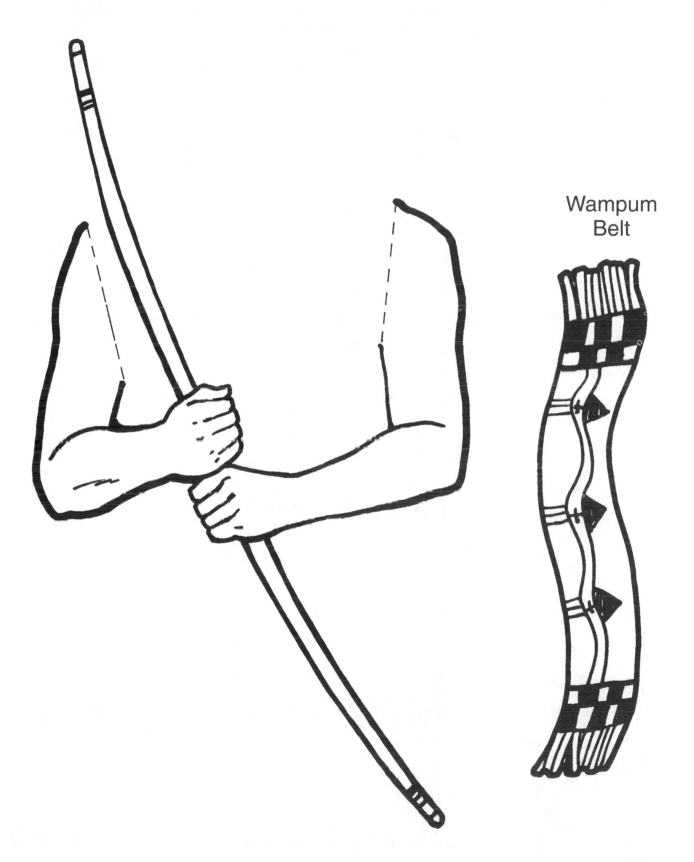

Wampum
Belt

Long House

The Iroquois of the Northeast lived in large, rectangular houses that had slanted or rounded roofs made of wood. Use pages 124–127 to create a paper model of a long house. Follow the directions for each section located at the top of each page. When completed, the long house will be 6" x 15" x 7". For best results, use sturdy paper. See picture of completed house on page 126.

Front and Back—Make two copies of page 124. One copy will be the front of the house, and the second copy will be the back of the house. Color and cut out the front and back of the house. Connect the front and back of the house to the walls at Tabs F. Connect Tabs A to the roof.

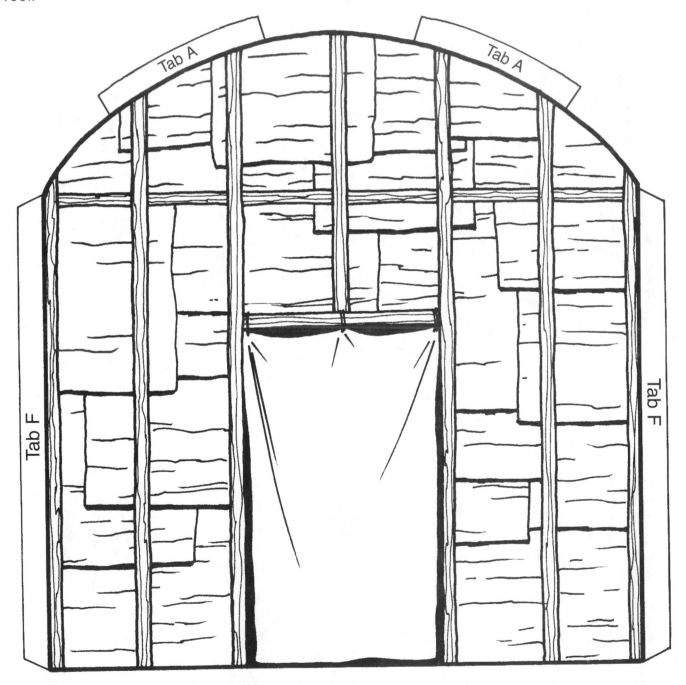

124

Long House *(cont.)*

Walls—Make four copies of the wall. Color and cut out each wall. Tape or glue two walls at Tab B to form one long wall. Cut off the other Tab B. Repeat for the other two walls. Connect each wall section to Tabs F located on the front and back section of the house.

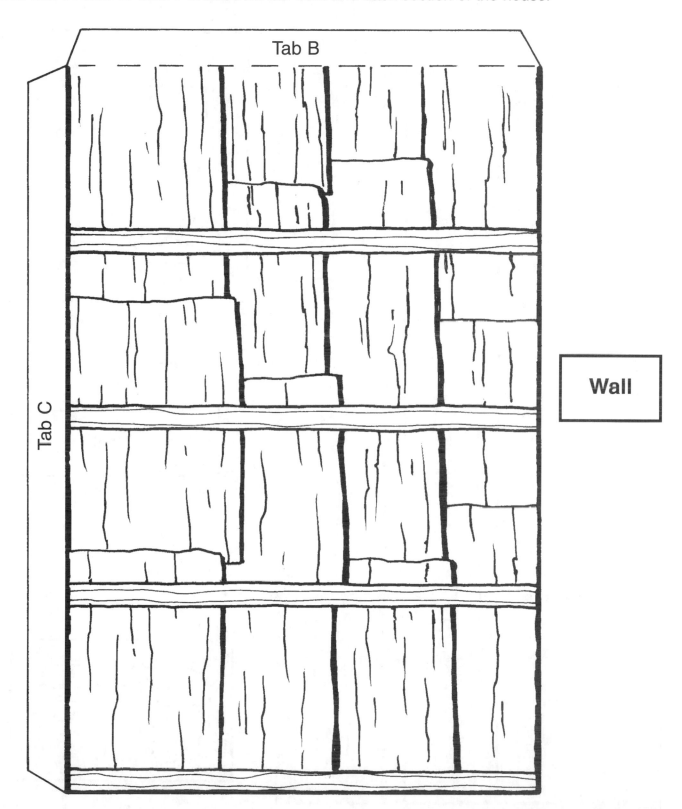

Long House (cont.)

Roof—Make two copies of page 126. Color and cut out pattern. Cut off one Tab D. Next, align Tab E on each section of the roof. Tape or glue the roofs together along the remaining Tab D. Connect section at Tab E to the other part of roof on page 127.

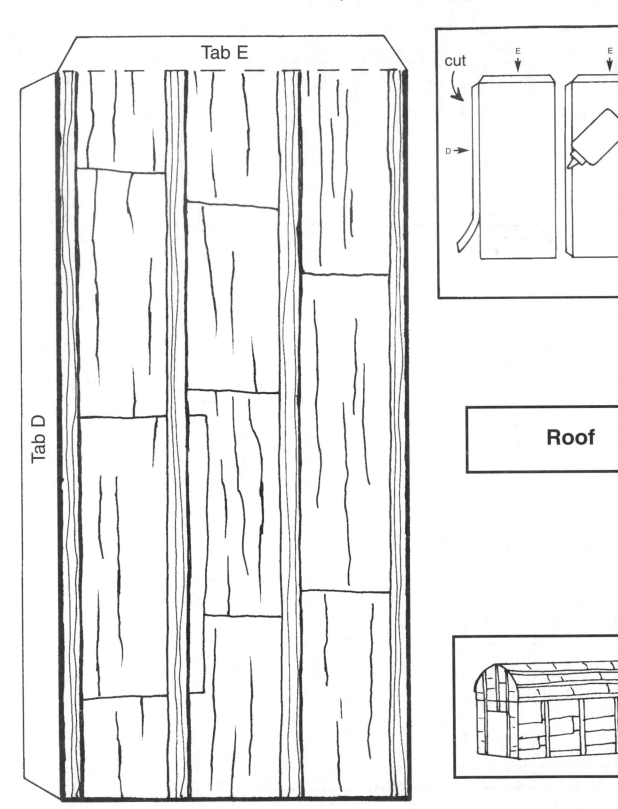

Roof

126

Long House *(cont.)*

Roof (cont.)—Make two copies of page 127. Color and cut out pattern. Cut off one Tab D. Tape or glue the roofs together along the remaining Tab D. Combine roof sections at Tab E. Attach the complete roof to the walls at Tabs C and to the front and back section of the house at Tabs A.

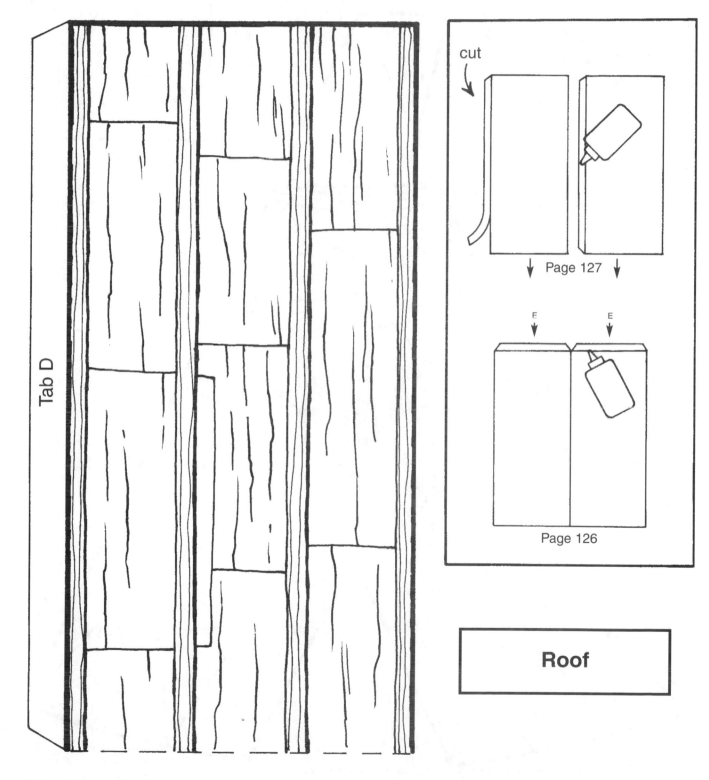

Roof

Tipi

Use pages 128–129.

The tipi was constructed from buffalo hides and used by the Plains people.

Color, then tape or glue the two halves together. Then role up in a cone to create a 3–D tipi.

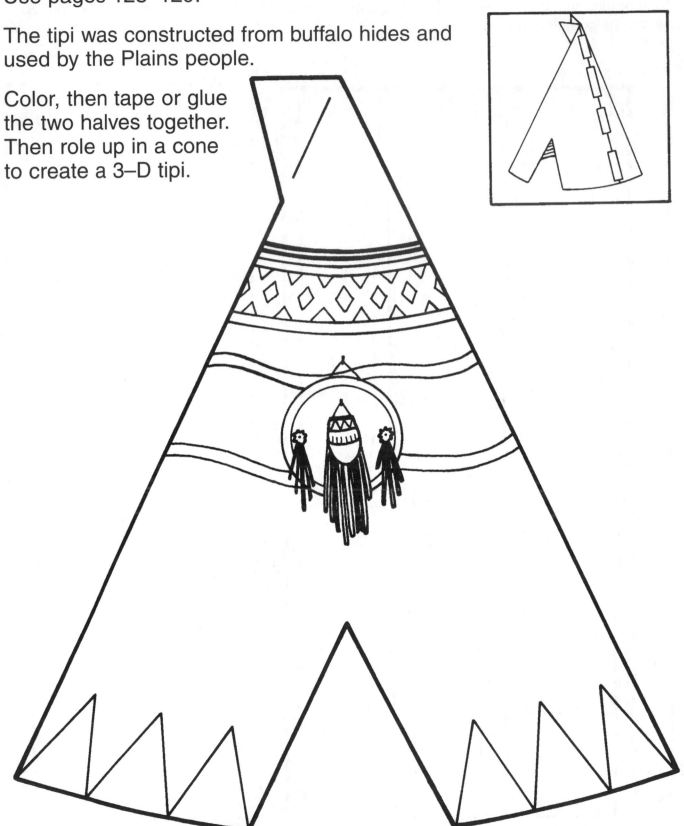

128

Tipi *(cont.)*

Pueblo

Use pages 130–131.

The people of the Southwest built adobe houses that were joined together like apartment buildings.

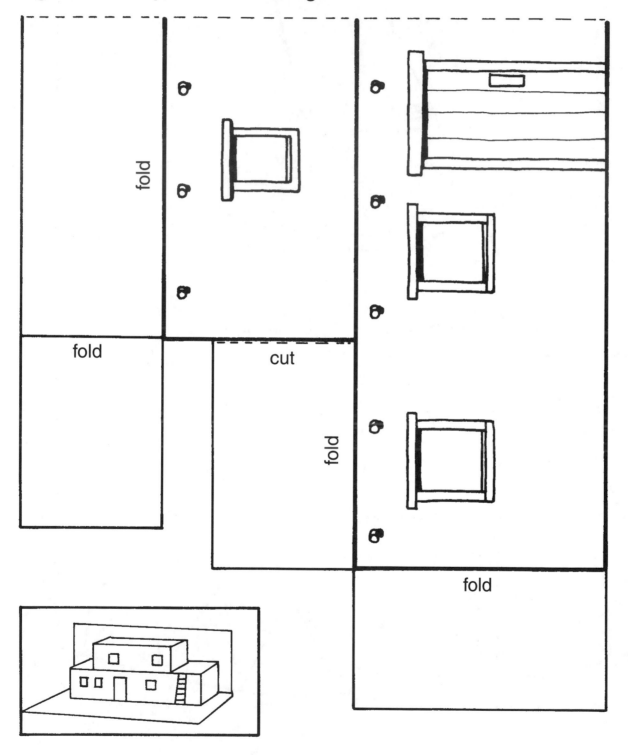

Pueblo *(cont.)*

Cut out and attach two sides of the pueblo at the tab. Fold the pueblo to match the diagram. Attach to a folded piece of tagboard to create back walls.

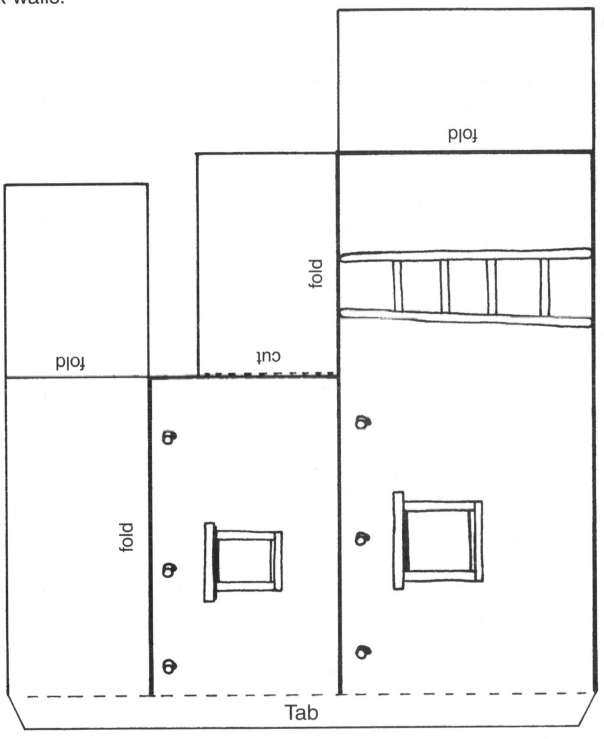

Scie..ce Patterns a..d Ideas

Have students assemble the flower as part of a study on plant parts. Identify the parts on real flowers, then use the Build a Flower patterns which show a cross section as a review. Discuss what plants need to grow, then assemble the Plant Needs pattern. Each leaf on this pattern depicts one of the things plants need to grow.

Use the weather patterns to create a word bank of weather words. Arrange words on raindrops or snowflakes around clouds and a rainbow. Have students create paper cloud pillows by stuffing the cloud pattern with newspaper. Glue tinsel to the bottom of the cloud to create falling rain. Have students color or paint a rainbow with the appropriate colors in order—red, orange, yellow, green, blue, indigo, and violet. Create a collage by gluing scraps of paper and magazine cutouts in the correct colors to the appropriate place on an enlarged rainbow. Weather patterns can also be used to record the weather of the day on a calendar or as shape books to record weather stories or weather poems.

Discuss life cycles with your students using the Stages of a Butterfly or the Stages of a Frog patterns. Make arrangements to actually observe these live animals in your classroom. Use the patterns as a preview of what will happen next or as a review of the entire process. Create a sequencing card for each of the stages, place them in a basket in the science area and see if the students can arrange them in order. Play What's Missing during circle time and remove one stage from each sequence. See who can tell you what stage has been removed. Decorate the pages of a book chronicling the observations the class makes throughout the life cycle studies.

Five familiar dinosaur patterns are given to enhance your dinosaur unit. Use them as story props, or prompts. Dinosaur patterns can also be used as part of a dinosaur timeline. Have children make and decorate their dinosaurs during art. Add sand or rice to the paint for texture. What color do they think dinosaurs might have been? Use the patterns on journal covers or as big books. Have students investigate and record their findings in these books. Create a poster for each dinosaur using the pattern and facts gathered by the students. Display them around the room and continue to add to them as new facts are learned.

Use the space shuttle and the astronaut to introduce your solar system unit.

Have students bring in a variety of recyclable items and create a sorting center using the recycling patterns. Attach a label and pattern to a cardboard box for each type of recyclable, then have students begin sorting. These boxes can also be used to collect and sort trash from the school yard. Be sure to discuss the importance of recycling and reusing the earth's resources.

As part of a unit on nutrition, you can have students make their own lunch boxes. Run two copies of the lunch box pattern for each student and staple together along bottom edge. Open the two halves like a book and glue in the various snack items. Discuss the food groups and the food pyramid and to which group each snack item belongs. Students can also label the food items.

Use the tooth as a book cover. Have students record tooth stories or poems or dental hygiene rules and why they are important. Use the toothpaste and toothbrush as part of a bulletin board display or as an art project. Encourage students to create new toothpaste flavors and write advertisements for them.

Discuss the five senses using the eye, ear, nose, tongue, and hand patterns. Set up different sensory stations in your science area. Use the patterns as labels for file folder activities. Create a bulletin board using the patterns as headers and illustrate with magazine pictures showing people using different senses.

Build a Flower

Use pages 133–135. See diagram for placement of flower parts.

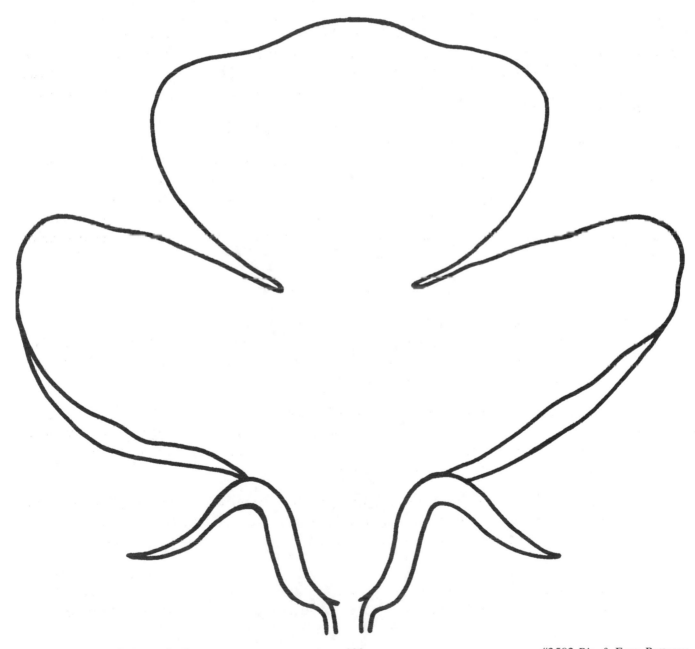

Build a Flower (cont.)

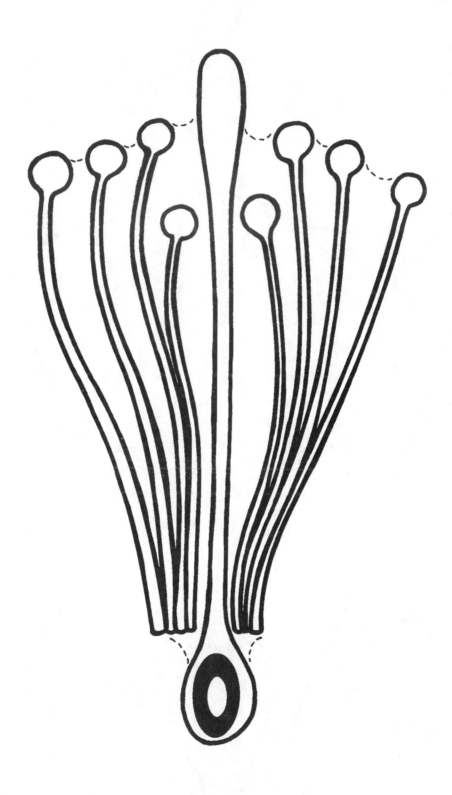

Build a Flower *(cont.)*

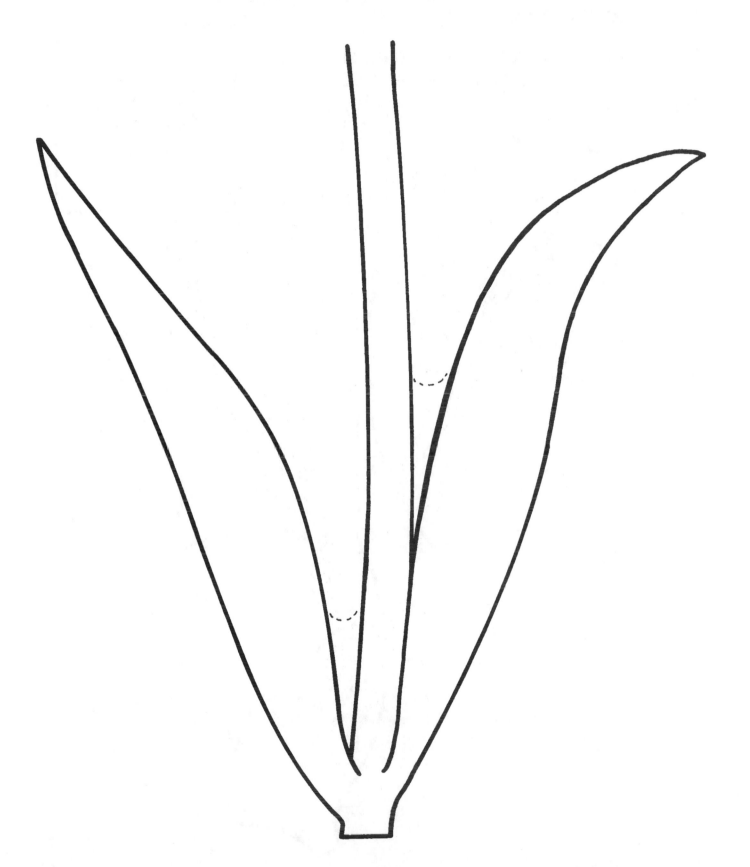

Plant Needs

Use pages 136–138.

Have students cut out, color, and label leaves *Sun* and *Water*. Attach the leaves to the plant on page 138.

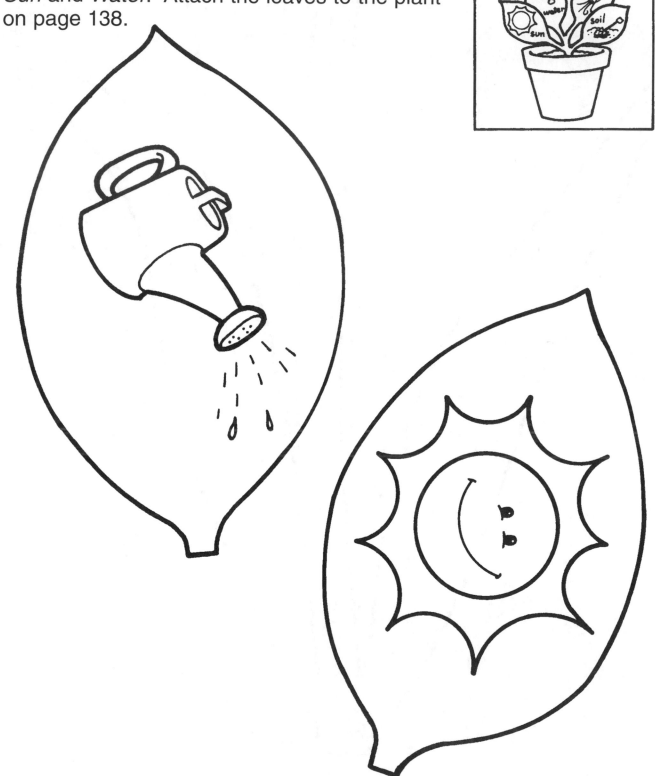

Plant Needs *(cont.)*

Have students cut out, color and label leaves *Air* and *Soil*. Attach to the plant on page 138.

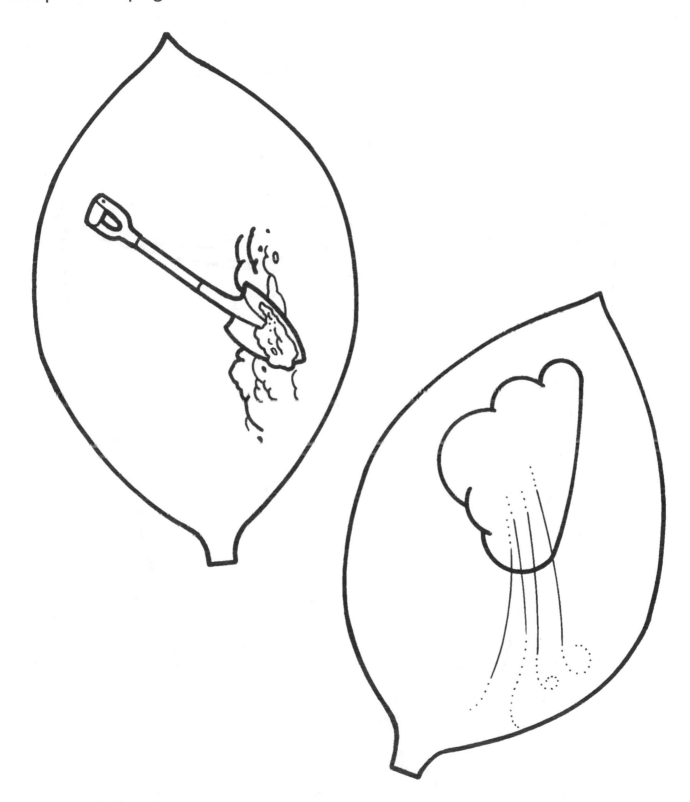

Plant Needs *(cont.)*

Attach the leaves from pages 136–137.

Sun

Wind

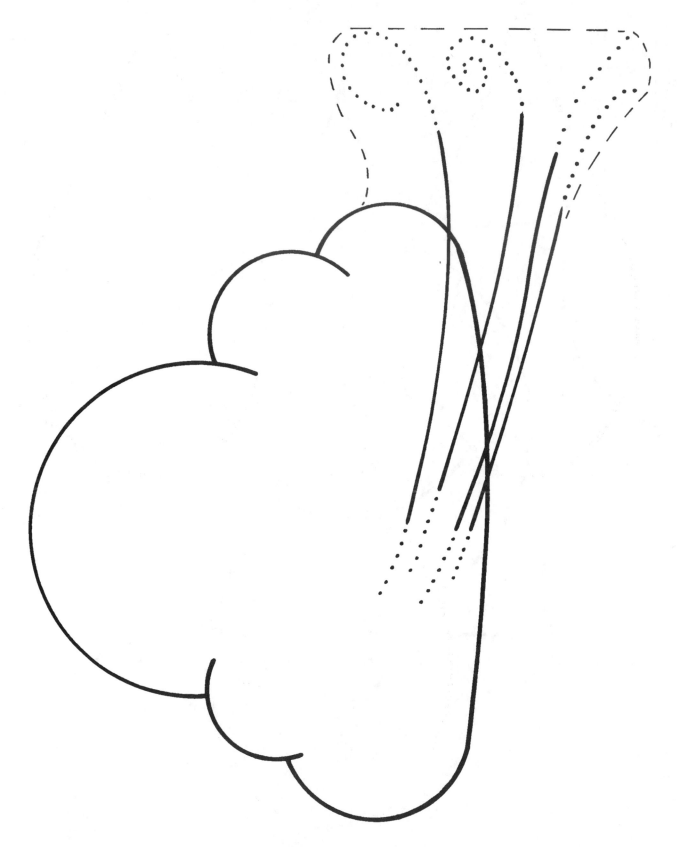

Rain

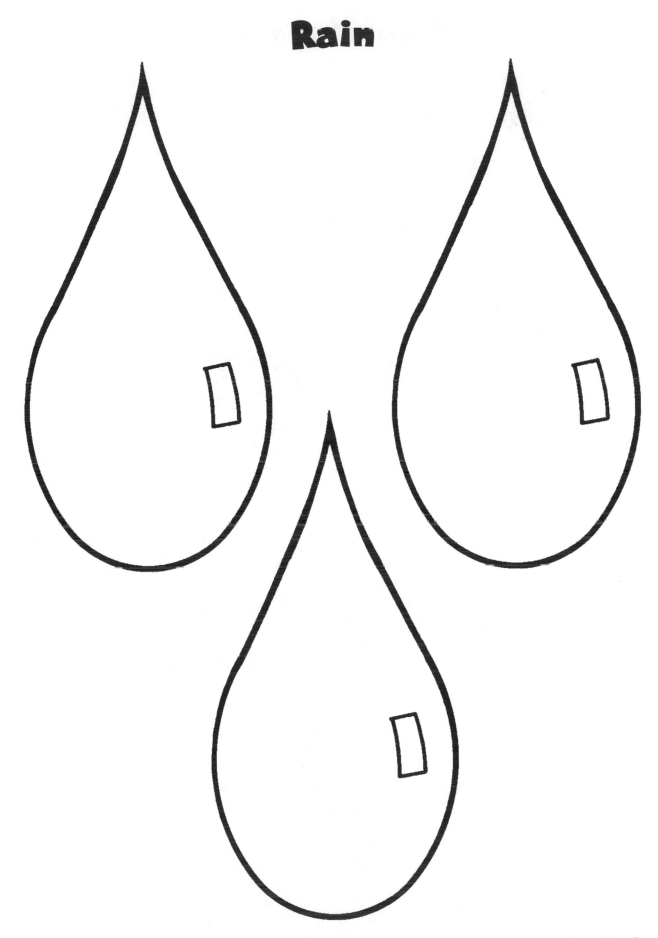

Snowflakes

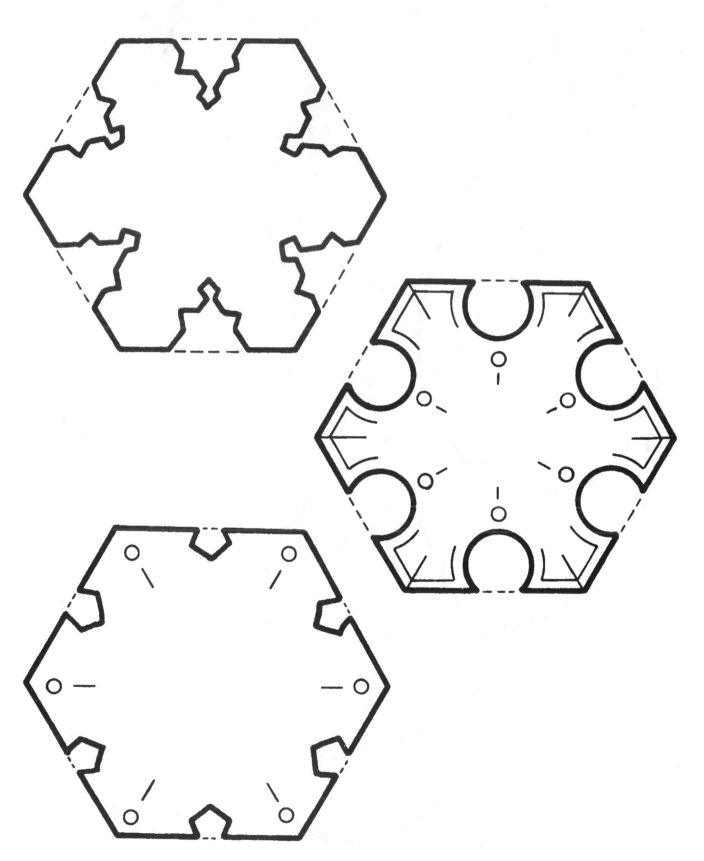

142

Cloud

Rainbow

Use pages 144–145. Connect the rainbow at the tab.

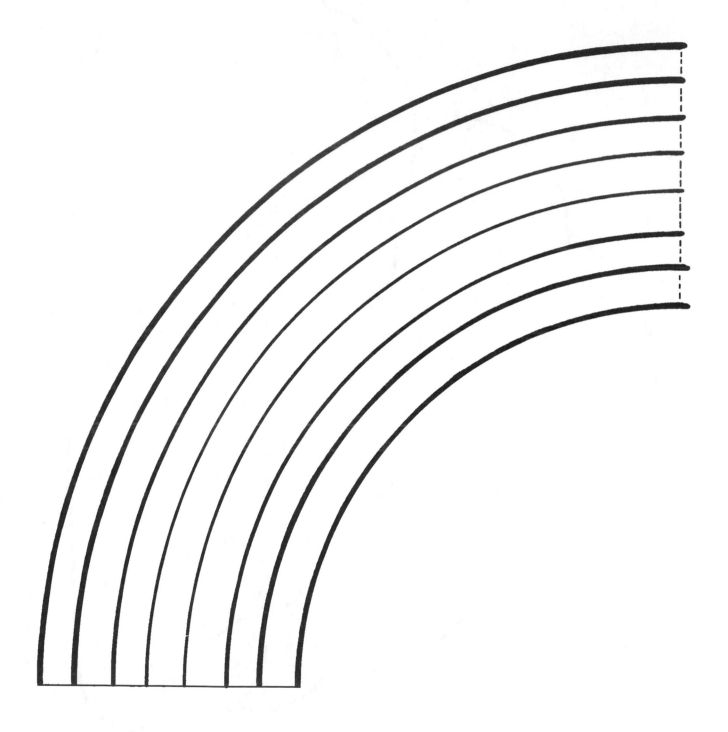

144

Rainbow *(cont.)*

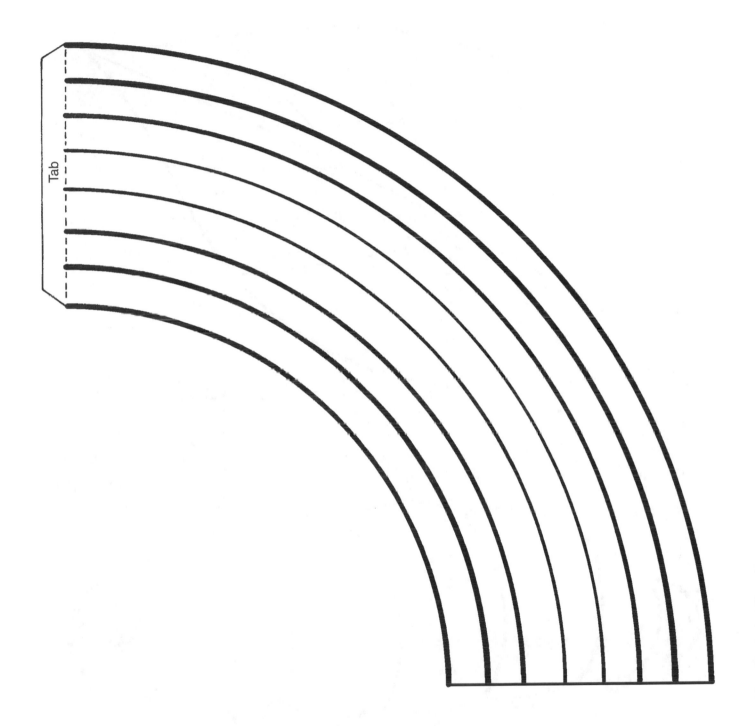

Tab

Stages of a Butterfly

Use pages 146–149.

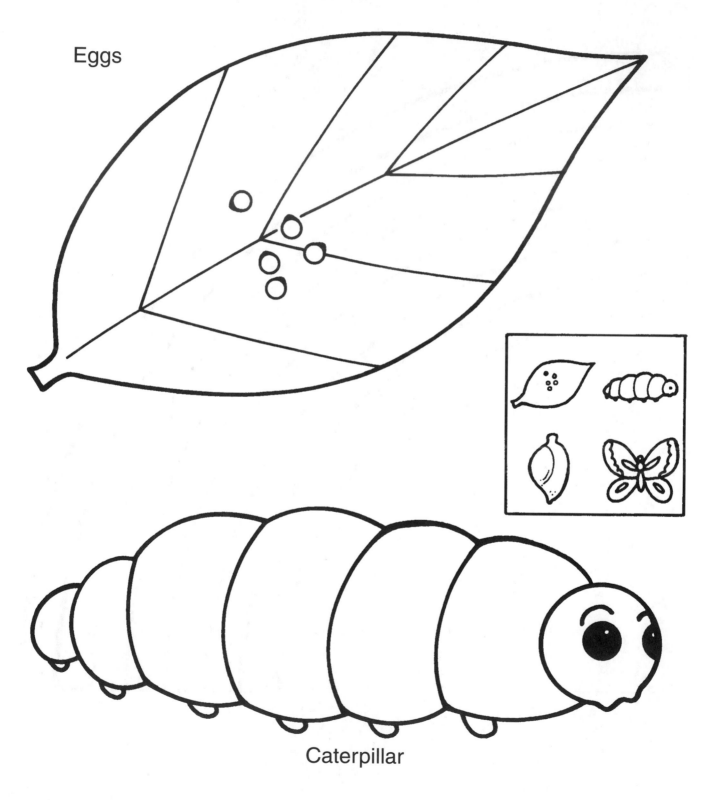

Eggs

Caterpillar

Stages of a Butterfly (cont.)

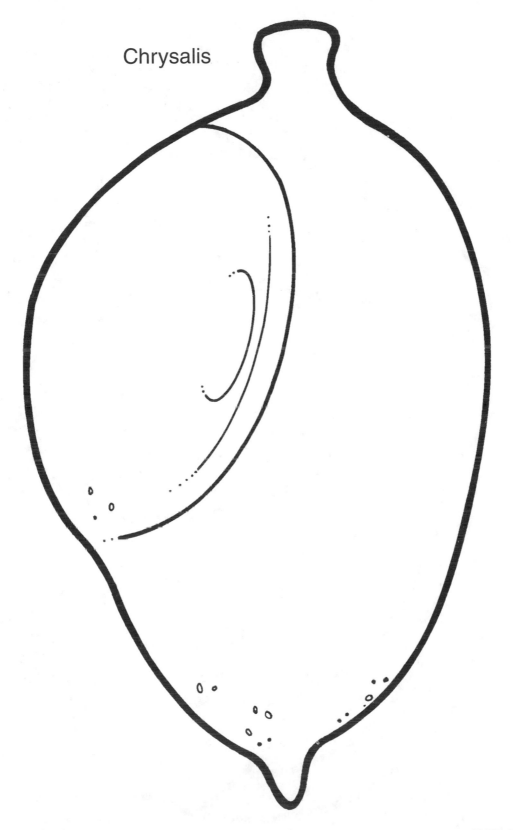

Chrysalis

Stages of a Butterfly (cont.)

Attach body A and right wing by
overlapping body A over body B
on page 149.

Right Wing

Body

A

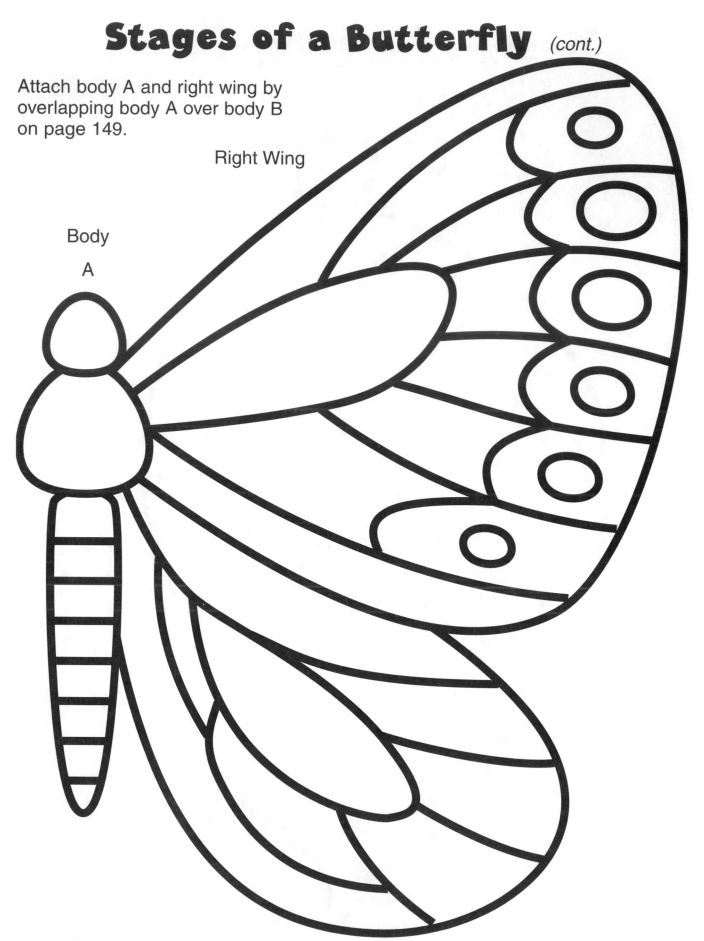

148

Stages of a Butterfly *(cont.)*

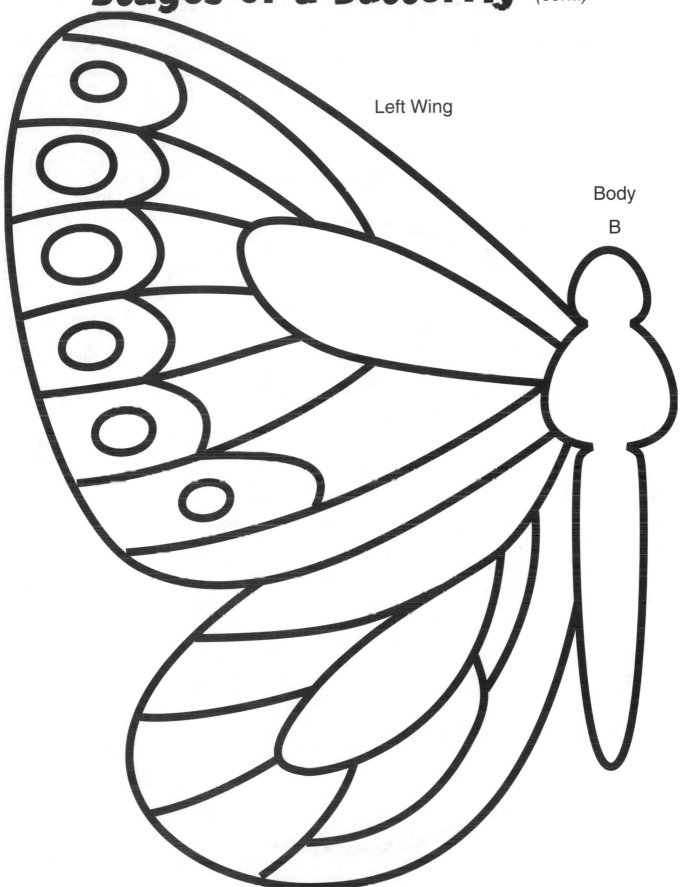

Left Wing

Body

B

Stages of a Frog

Use pages 150–153.

Egg Cluster

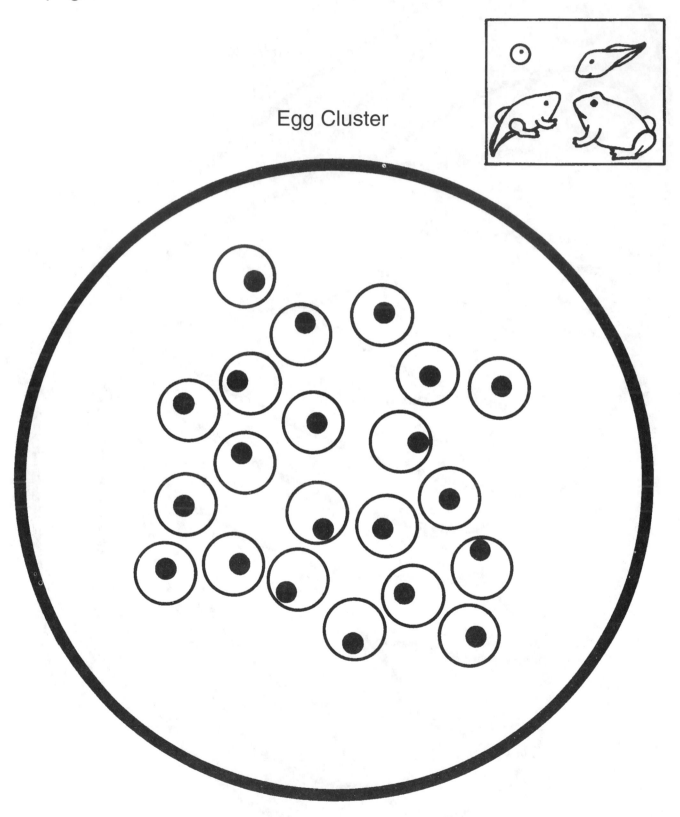

Stages of a Frog *(cont.)*

Tadpole

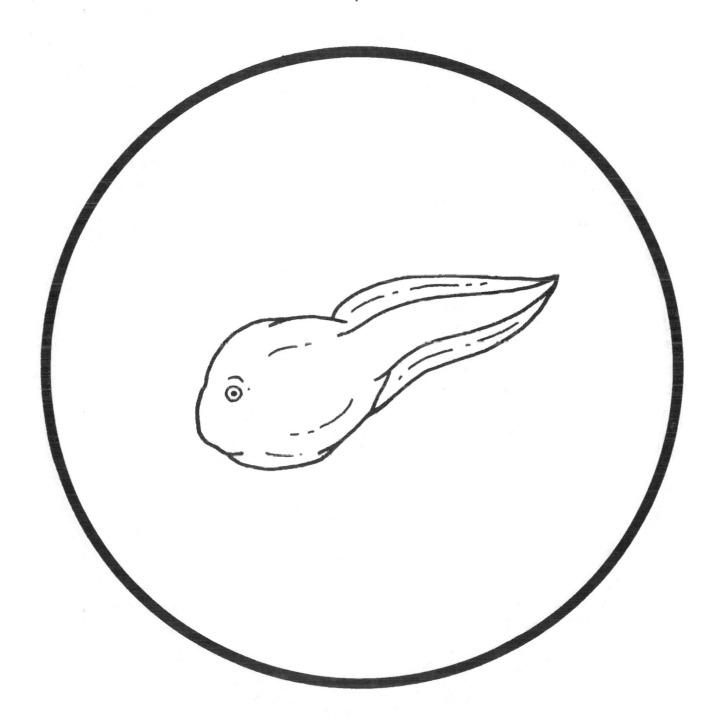

Stages of a Frog (cont.)

Tadpole with Emerging Legs

Stages of a Frog *(cont.)*

Frog

Tyrannosaurus Rex

Use pages 154–156. Attach head to torso at Tab A. Attach tail to torso at Tab B.

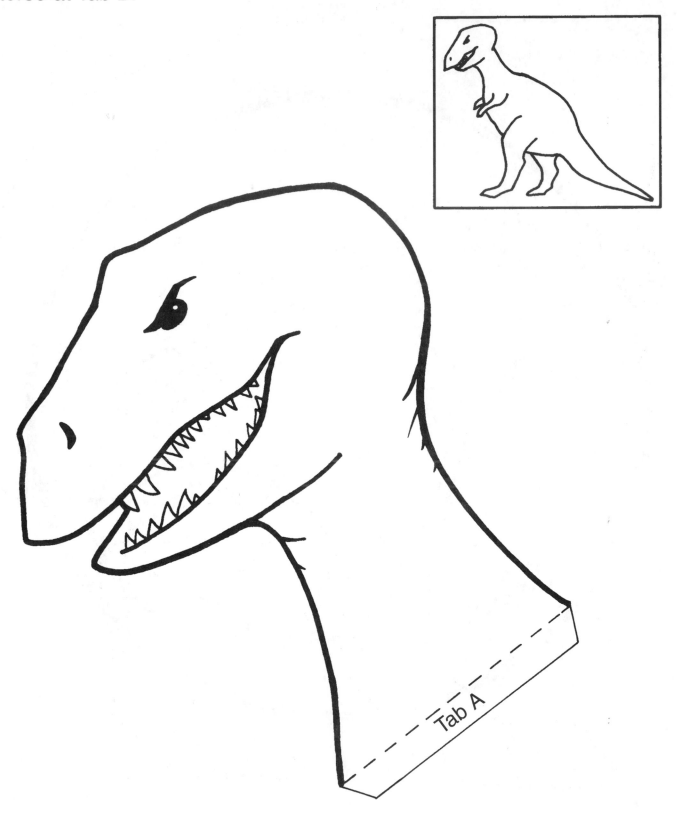

Tab A

Tyrannosaurus Rex *(cont.)*

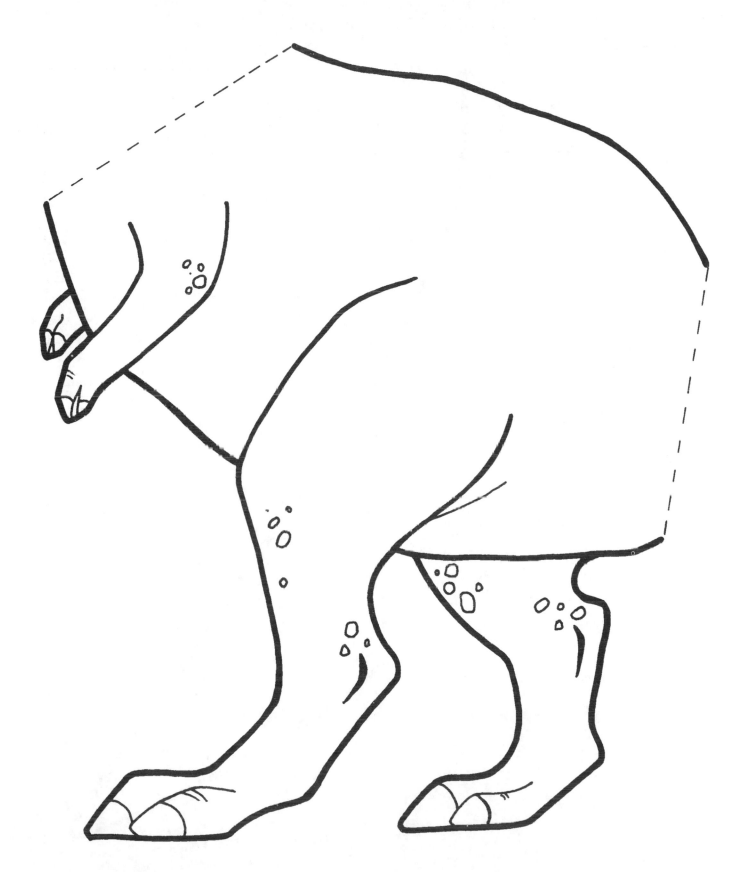

Tyrannosaurus Rex *(cont.)*

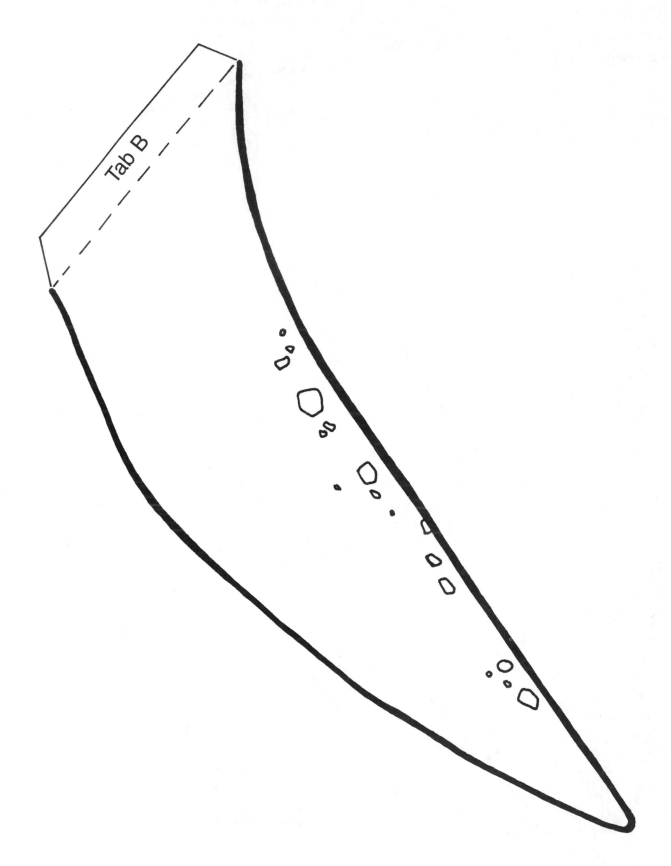

Tab B

156

Science

Triceratops

Use pages 157–159. Attach the head to the torso at Tab A. Attach the tail to the torso at Tab B.

Triceratops *(cont.)*

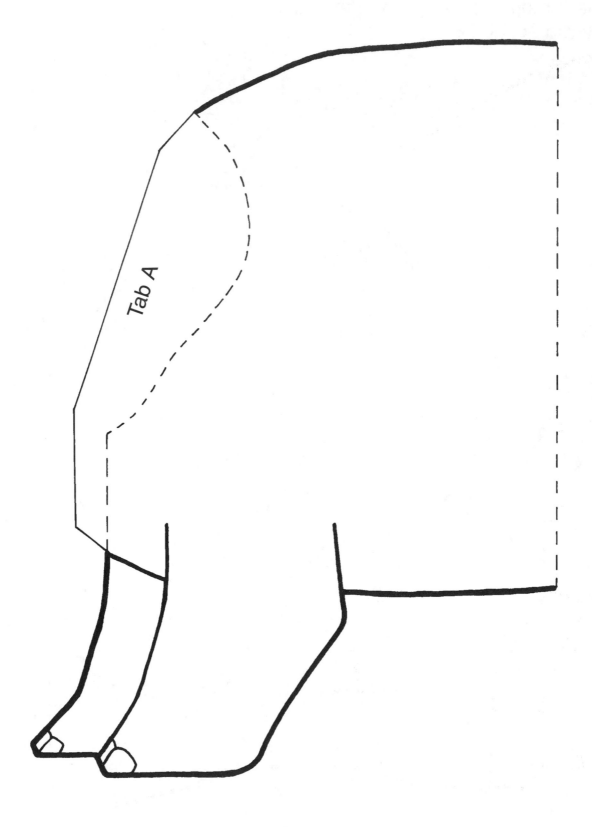

Tab A

Triceratops *(cont.)*

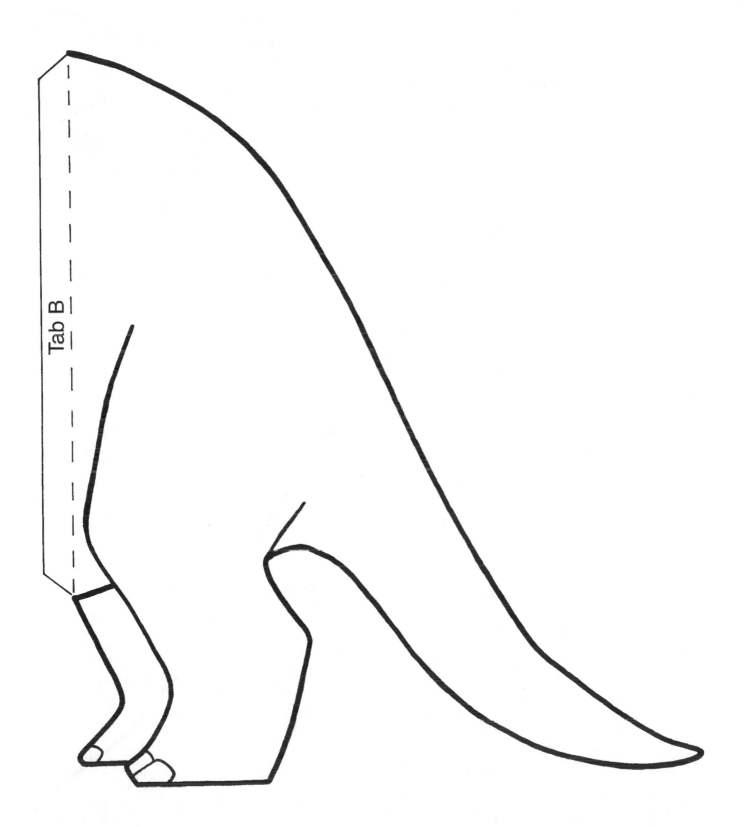

Tab B

Apatosaurus

Use pages 160–162. Attach the head to the torso at Tab A. Attach the tail to the torso at Tab B.

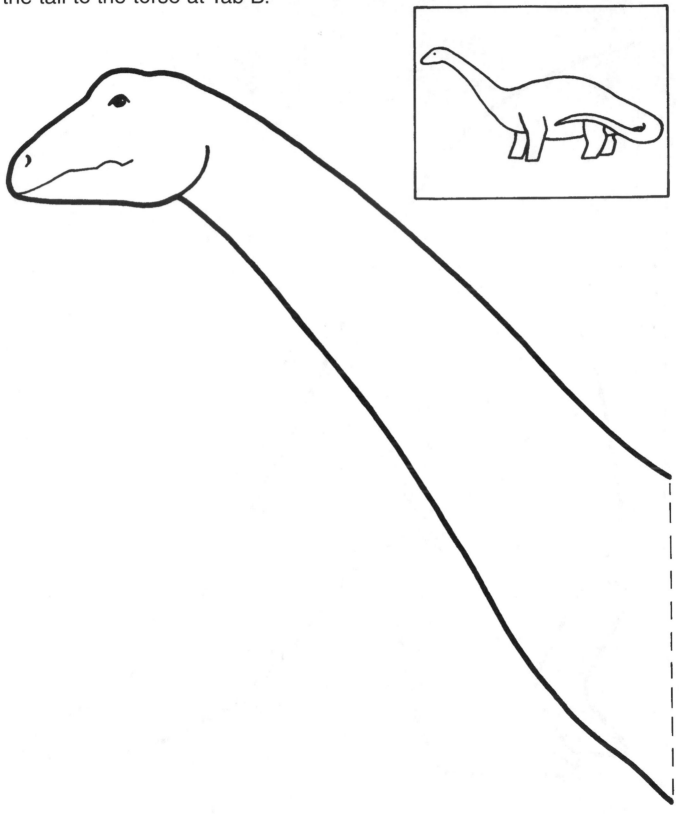

Apatosaurus *(cont.)*

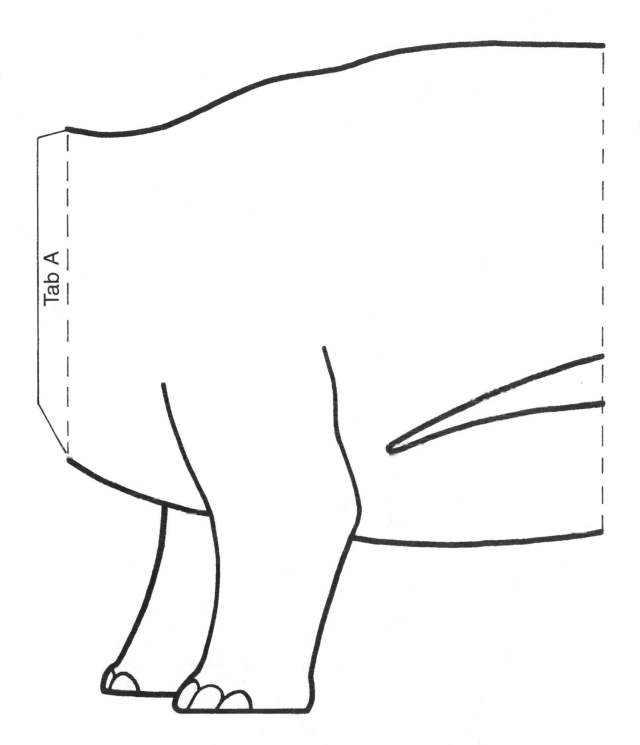

Apatosaurus (cont.)

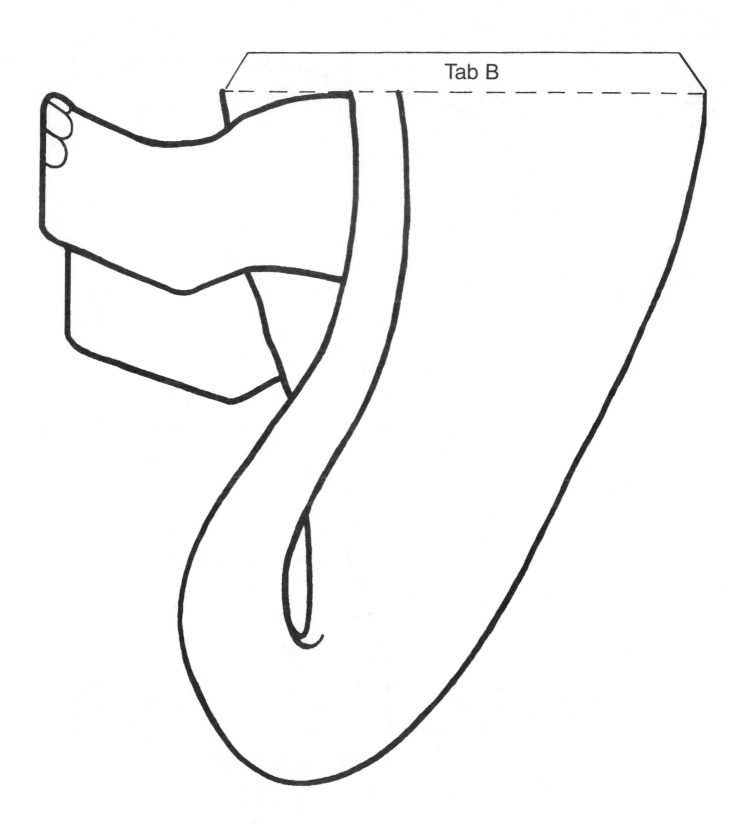

Tab B

Pteranodon

Use pages 163–164. Attach the left wing to the torso at Tab A. Attach the right wing to the torso at Tab B.

Pteranodon *(cont.)*

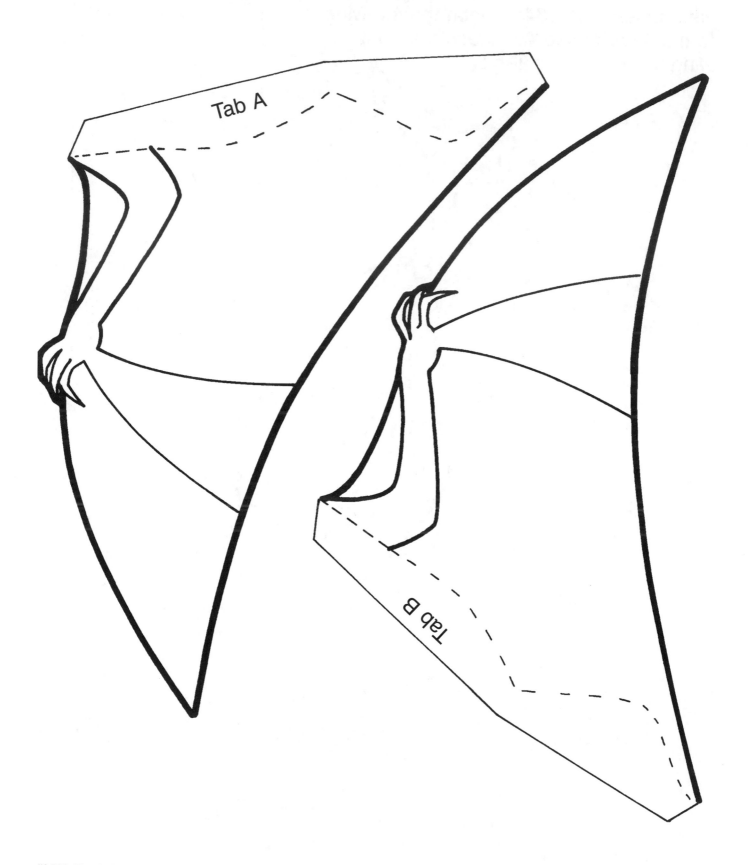

Stegosaurus

Use pages 165–167. Attach the head to the torso at Tab A. Attach the tail to the torso at Tab B.

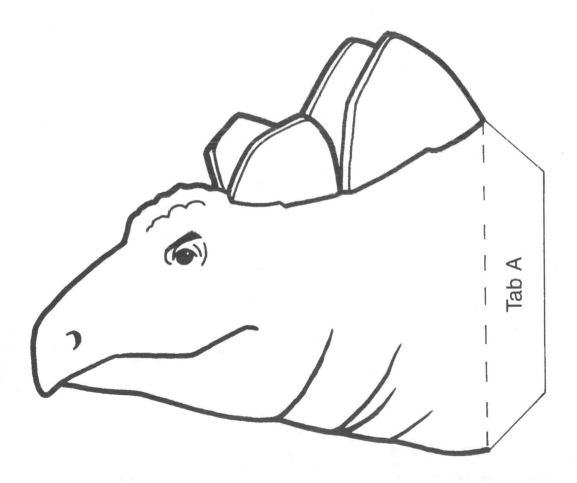

Tab A

Stegosaurus (cont.)

Stegosaurus *(cont.)*

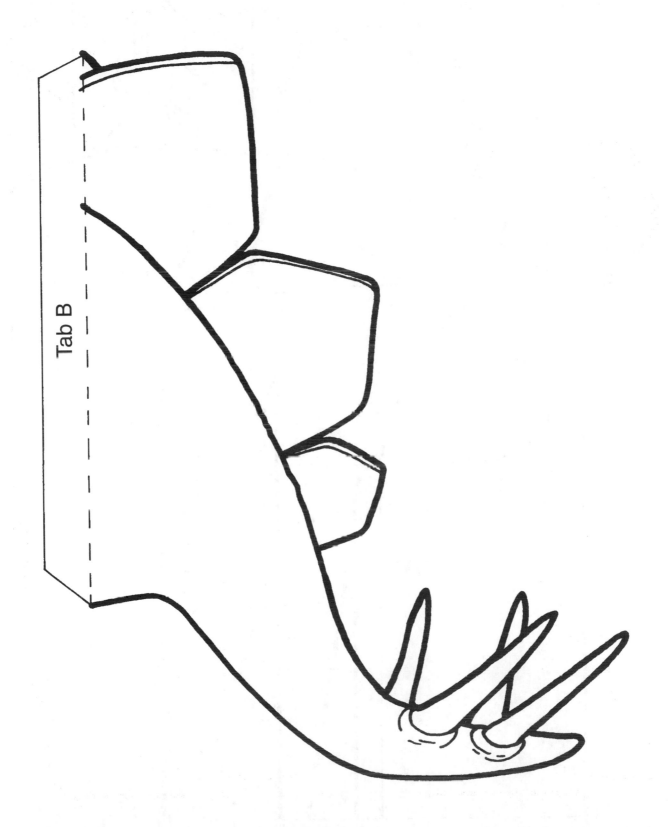

Tab B

Space Shuttle

Use pages 168–169. Cut out the shuttle and connect at the tab.

Space Shuttle *(cont.)*

Tab

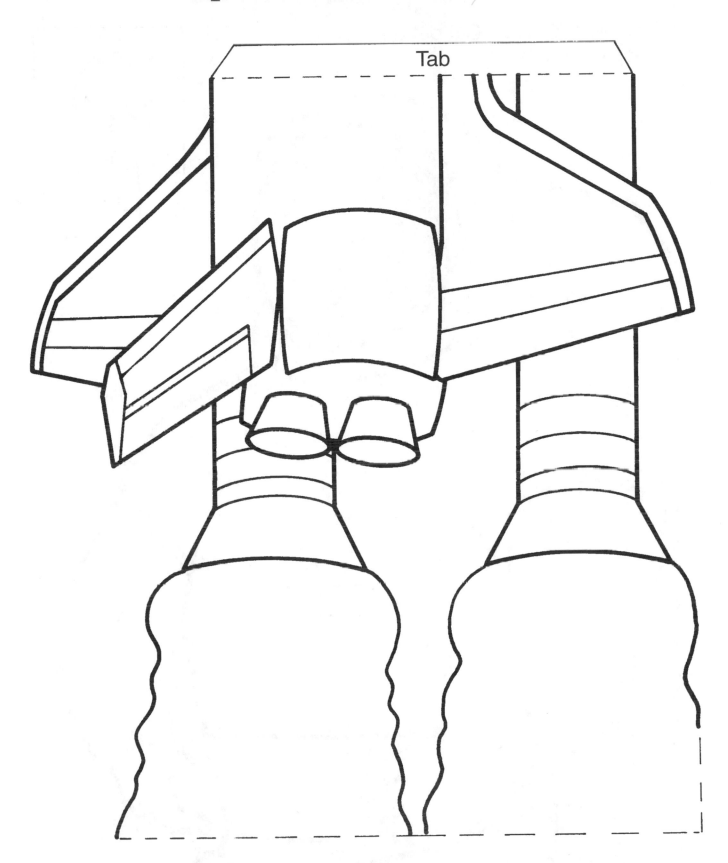

Astronaut

Use pages 170–171. Cut out and
connect at the tab.

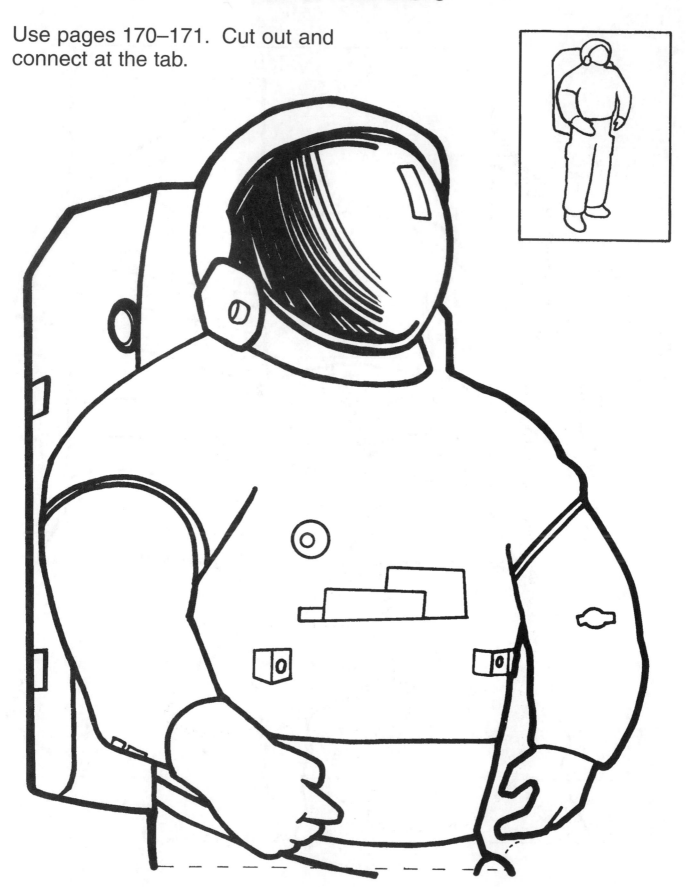

Astronaut *(cont.)*

Tab

Recycling

Use pages 172–174.

Newspapers

Cardboard

Milk Jug

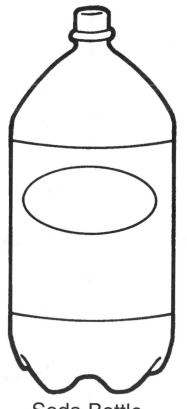

Soda Bottle

Recycling (cont.)

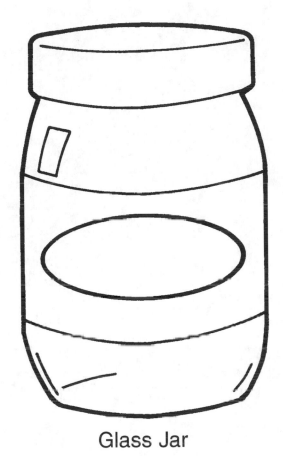

Glass Jar

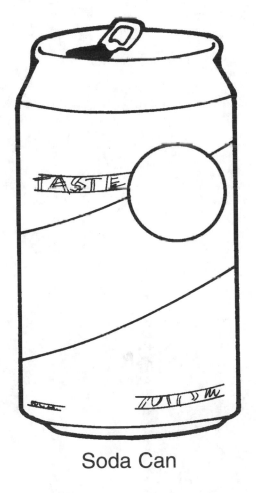

Soda Can

Recycling Labels

Glass

Cans

Plastic

Metal

Lunch Box

Use pages 175–177. Make two lunch boxes per student. Cut out the lunch boxes and tape them together at the bottom.

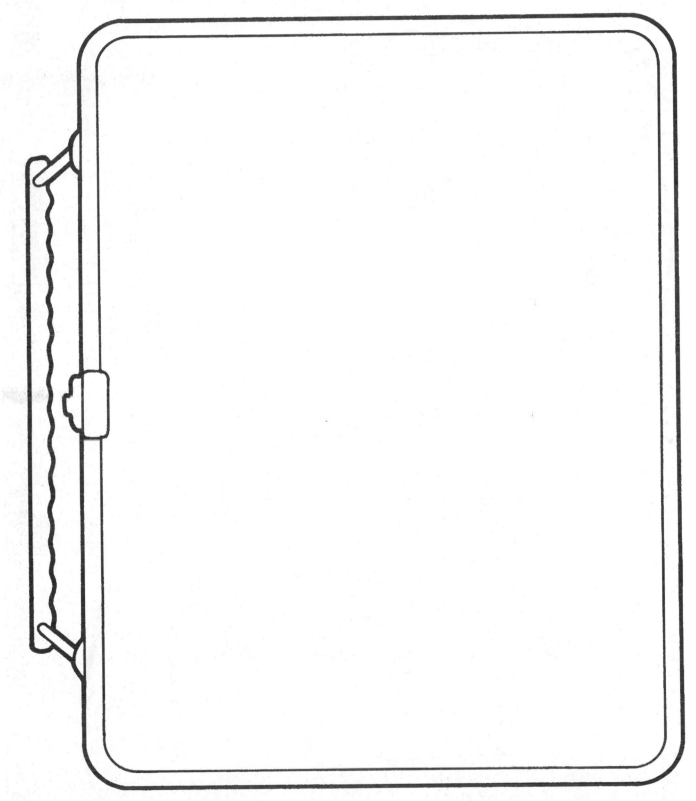

Snacks

Copy pages 176–177 for each student to use with the lunch box on page 175.

Snacks *(cont.)*

Copy pages 176–177 for each student to use with the lunch box on page 175.

Food Pyramid

Use pages 178–179. Cut out and connect at the tab.

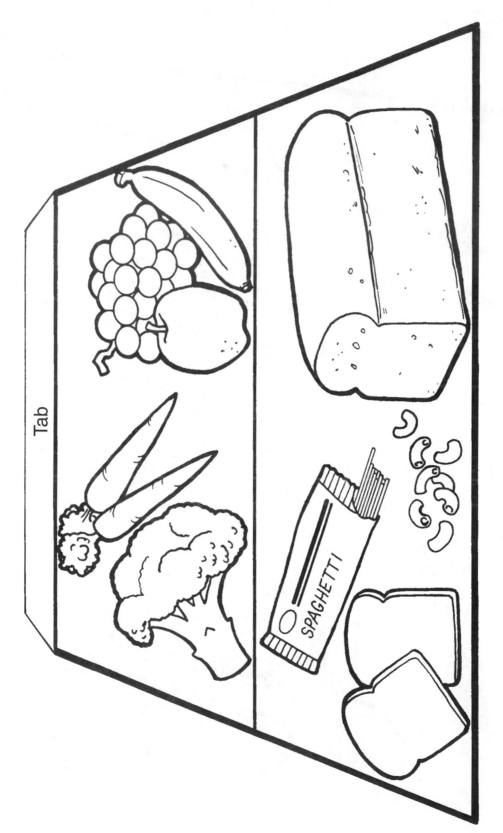

Tab

SPAGHETTI

178

Food Pyramid (cont.)

Tooth

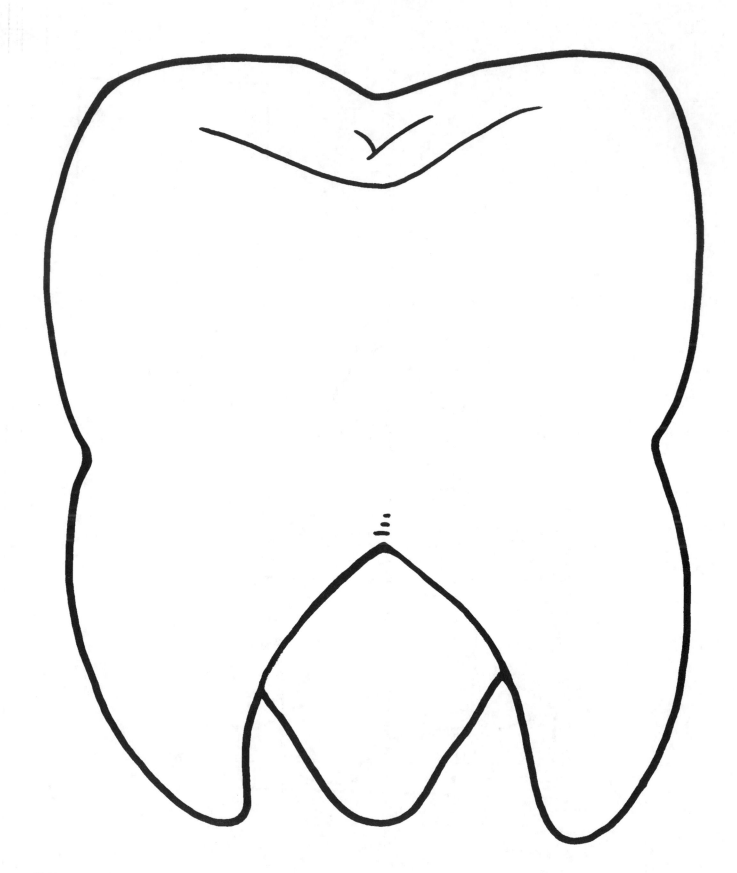

Toothbrush

Cut out and connect at the tab.

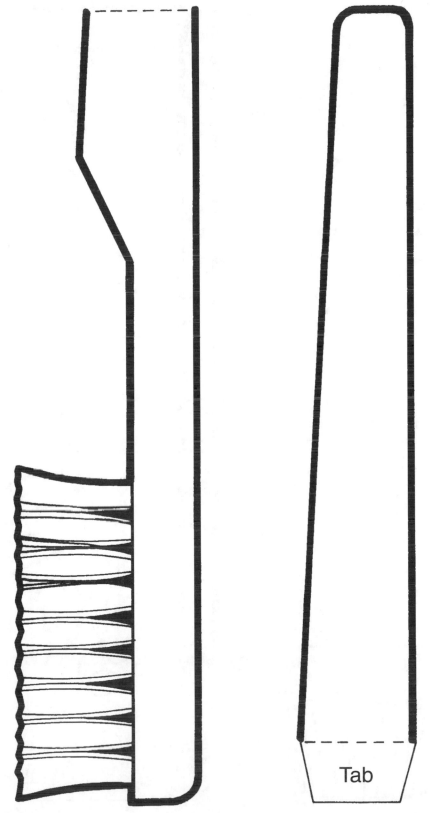

Tab

Toothpaste

Cut out and connect at the tab.

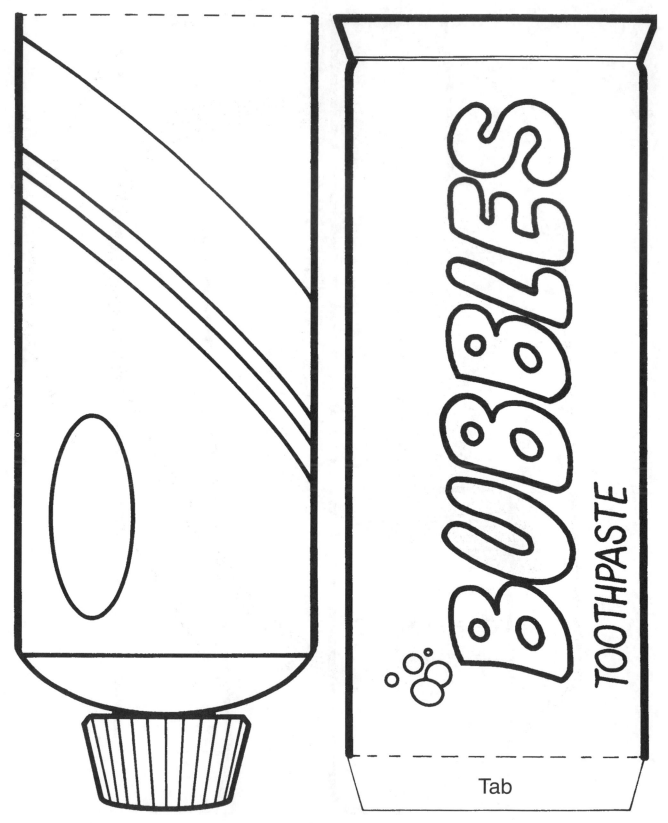

Tab

182   © *Teacher Created Materials, Inc.*

Five Senses

Ear

Five Senses (cont.)

Nose

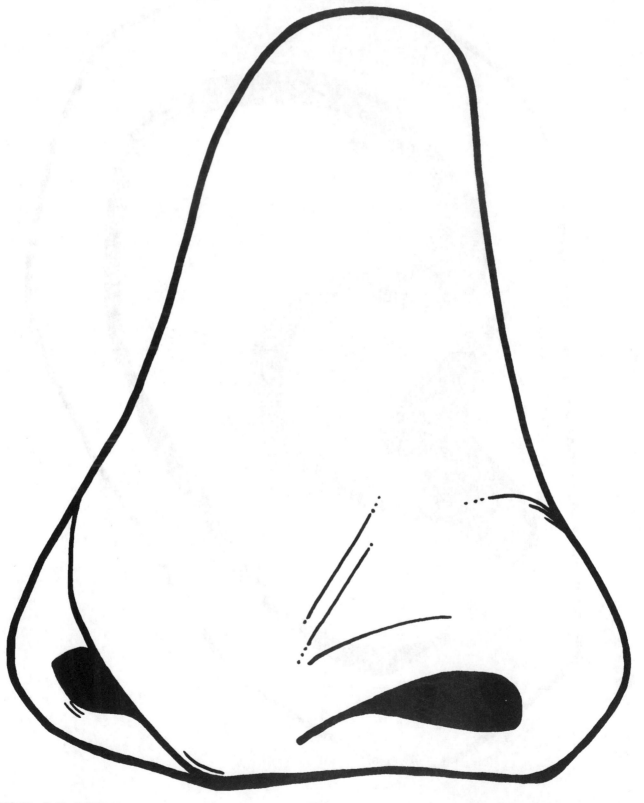

Five Senses *(cont.)*

Eye

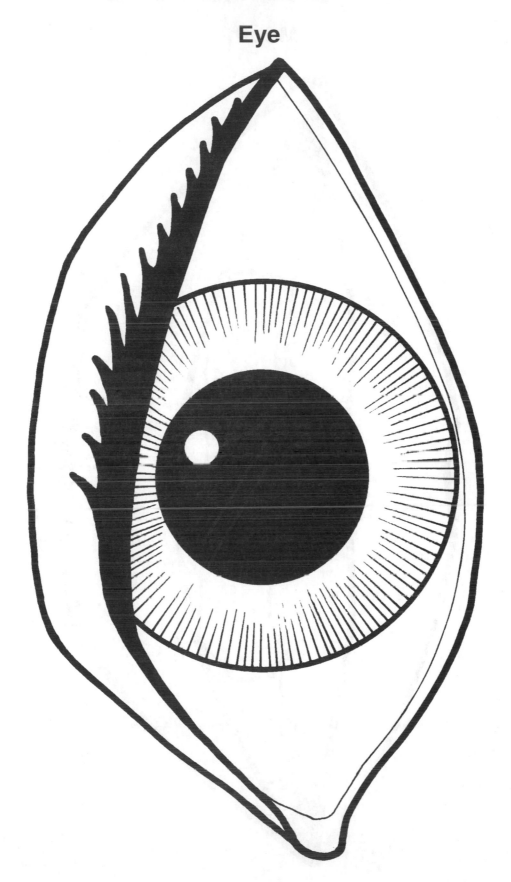

Five Senses *(cont.)*

Mouth

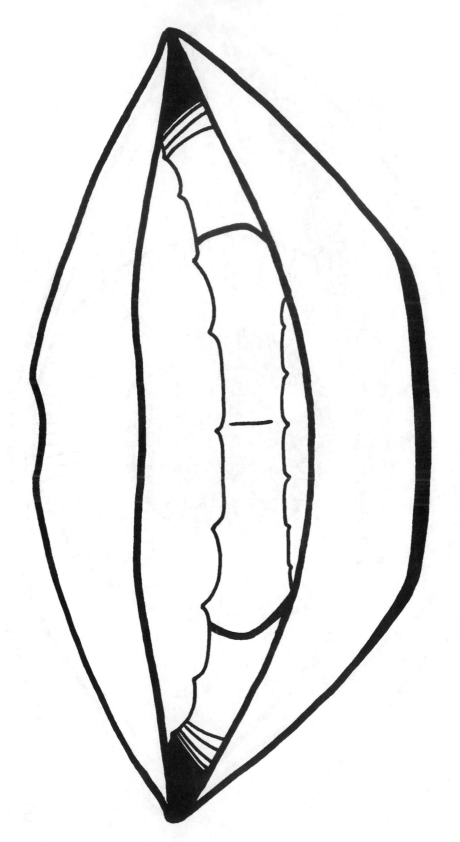

      186   © *Teacher Created Materials, Inc.*

Five Senses *(cont.)*

Hand

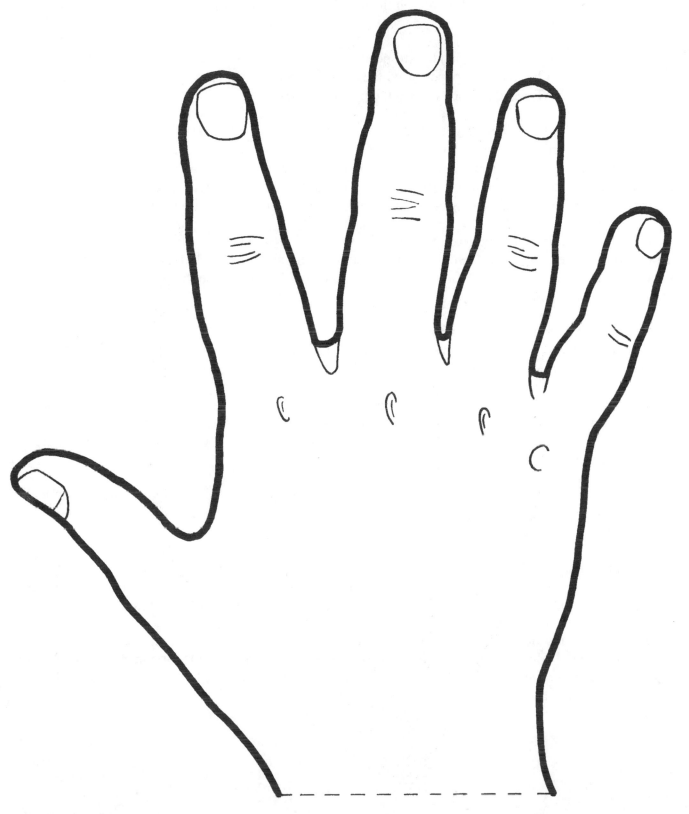

Math Patterns and Ideas

Use the two different types of clocks to enhance your study of time. Students can construct the analog clock with moveable hands and use it to show times or to figure out time story problems in the math center. Color and cut out the digital clock, laminate it, and use it in the math center with a dry erase marker or grease pencil. Students can read the time on the analog clock and record it on the digital clock, or vice versa.

Use the morning, noon, and night patterns to generate discussion of what is generally done at each of those times. Create a list on chart paper or on the board, then have students write a story or poem for each time of the day. Record in books using the patterns as covers.

Use the math symbols to decorate your math center. Create another set of symbols for use with manipulatives. Color, cut out, and laminate these symbols, then have students arrange the manipulatives and symbols to create number sentences. Numeral patterns can also be used to label these number sentences. Students can create number books using the numeral patterns as book covers. The numeral patterns can be used as coloring sheets or as counting cards in the math center.

Create your own set of dominoes using the domino pattern and sticky dots. Use a different color for each number. For example, all "five" dominoes could be red, and you would have one domino depicting 0 and 5, one showing 1 and 4, and another showing 2 and 3. Use the the dominoes in the math center to practice fact families.

Use the graph grid to create your own graphs. Label the bottom with items to be graphed, then graph away! Have students generate their own ideas for graphs, collect data, and then create graphs. Collect all graphs together in a class graph book or display on the bulletin board.

Practice fractions using the pizza, apple, pie, and candy bar patterns. The pizza is marked into eighths, the apple is divided into fourths, the pie is marked in sixths, and the candy bar is divided into sixteenths. Each student can create his or her own set of fraction pieces or you can create a laminated set for the math center.

Have the students design classroom coins and dollar bills to help learn about counting money. Have them use standard denominations. Make the cash register and have one student pretend to be the cashier while another student pretends to be the shopper.

Set up an imaginary store in your math center. You can put prices on real items and store them in a learning center box or create a file folder with magazine cutouts and prices. This idea can also be used to create a menu for a restaurant. Have students practice purchasing items and making change.

Students can use the ruler pattern to construct their own rulers for measuring. The ruler can also be used to decorate the edge of a math bulletin board. Decorate a board with the tape measure pattern and attach a length of sewing tape to it. The pint and quart patterns can be used to show the relationship between the two and as part of the measuring bulletin board.

Analog Clock

Use pages 189–190. For best results, use heavy paper and laminate the assembled clock and hands. Attach the hands using a paper fastener or brad to allow movement.

Analog Clock (cont.)

Digital Clock

Laminate the clock to be used with a grease pencil or dry erase marker.

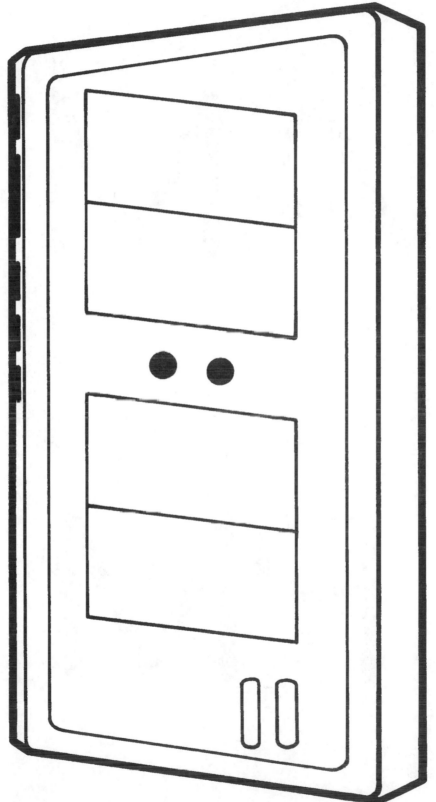

AM/PM Labels

AM

PM

Morning

Noon

Night

Symbols

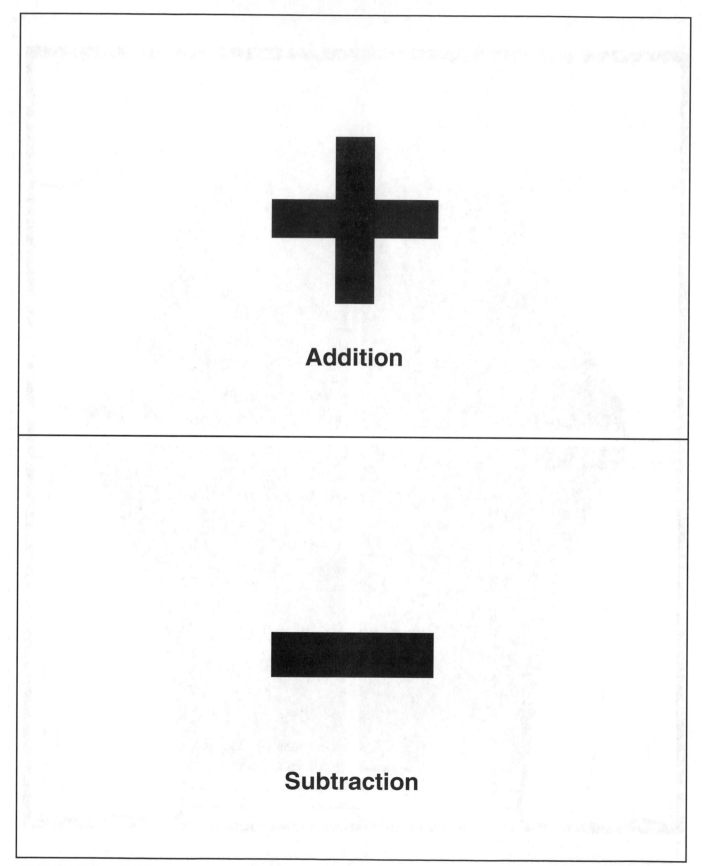

Addition

Subtraction

Symbols *(cont.)*

Multiplication

Division

Numerals

Zero

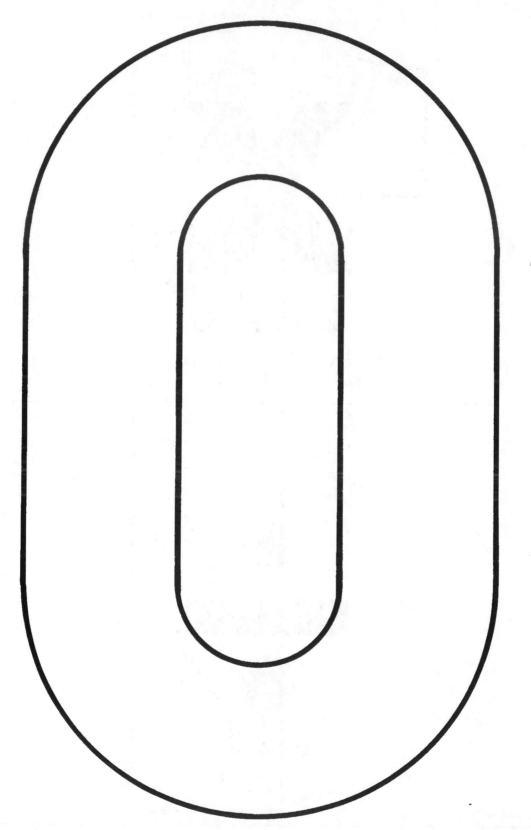

Numerals *(cont.)*

One

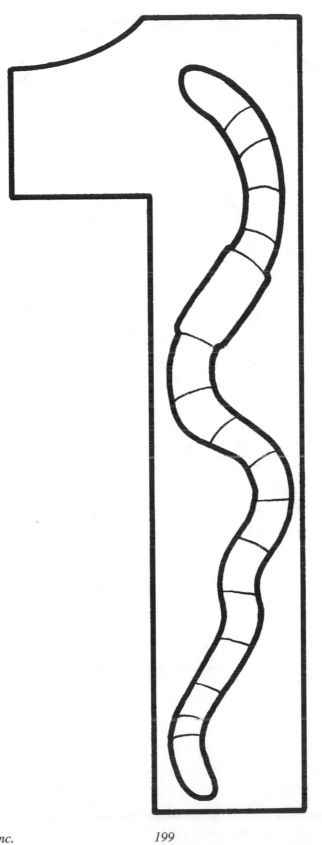

Numerals *(cont.)*

Two

Numerals *(cont.)*

Three

Numerals *(cont.)*

Four

Numerals *(cont.)*

Five

Numerals *(cont.)*

Six

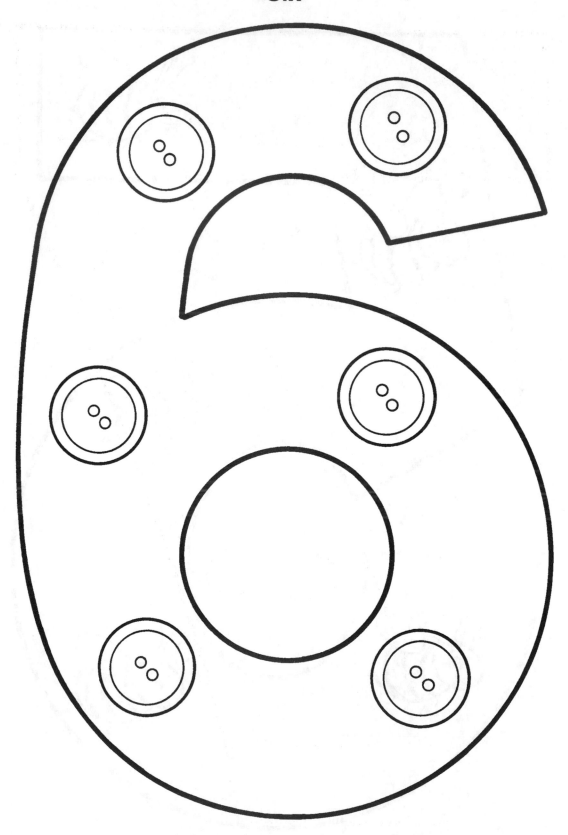

Numerals *(cont.)*

Seven

Numerals *(cont.)*

Eight

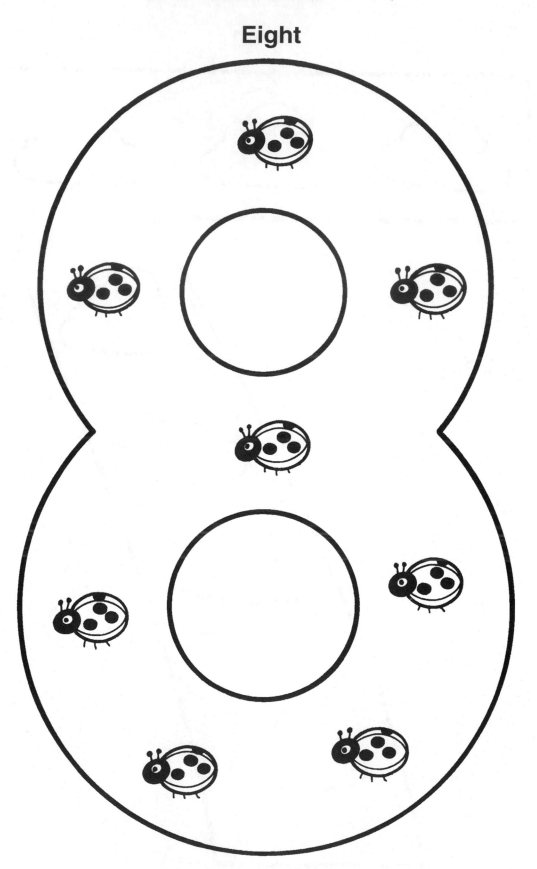

Numerals *(cont.)*

Nine

Domino

Use sticky dots to show number value.

Graph Grid

Use pages 209–210. Cut out the graph and connect at the tab.

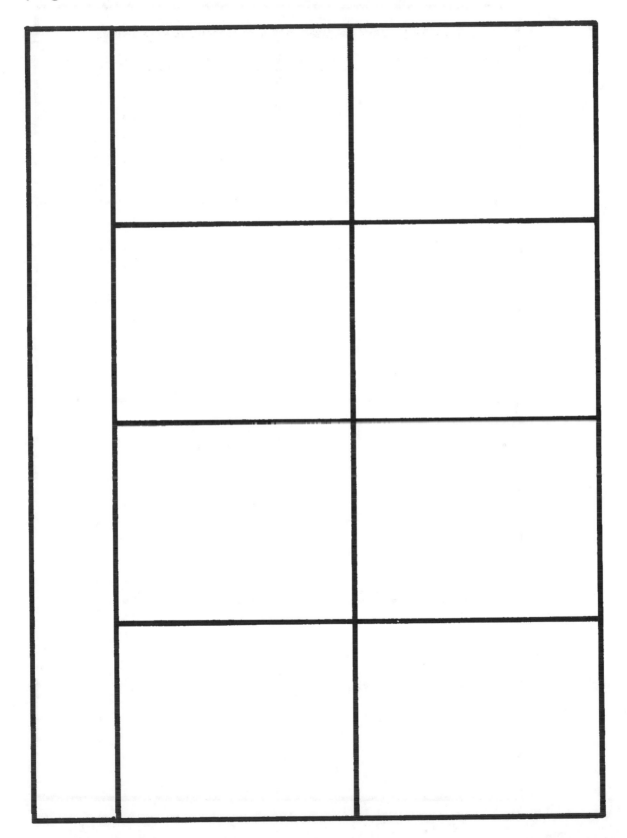

Graph Grid *(cont.)*

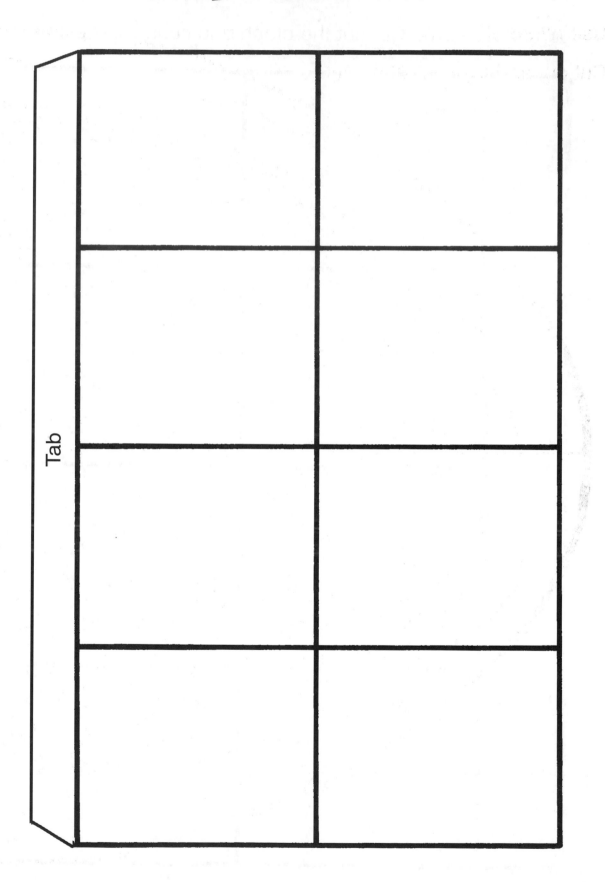

Pizza Fractions

Use pages 211–212.

Cut out and connect at the tab.

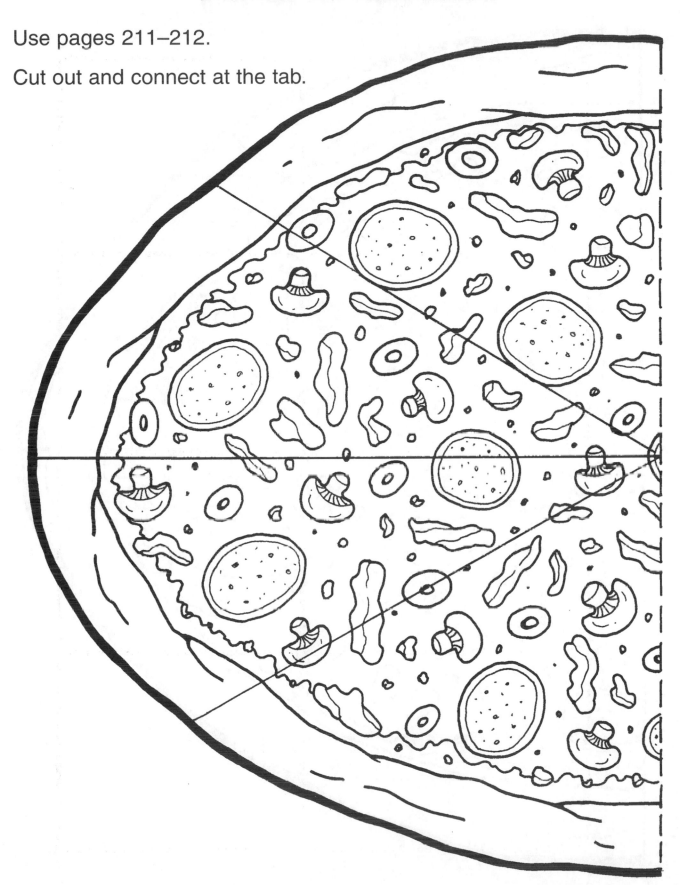

Pizza Fractions (cont.)

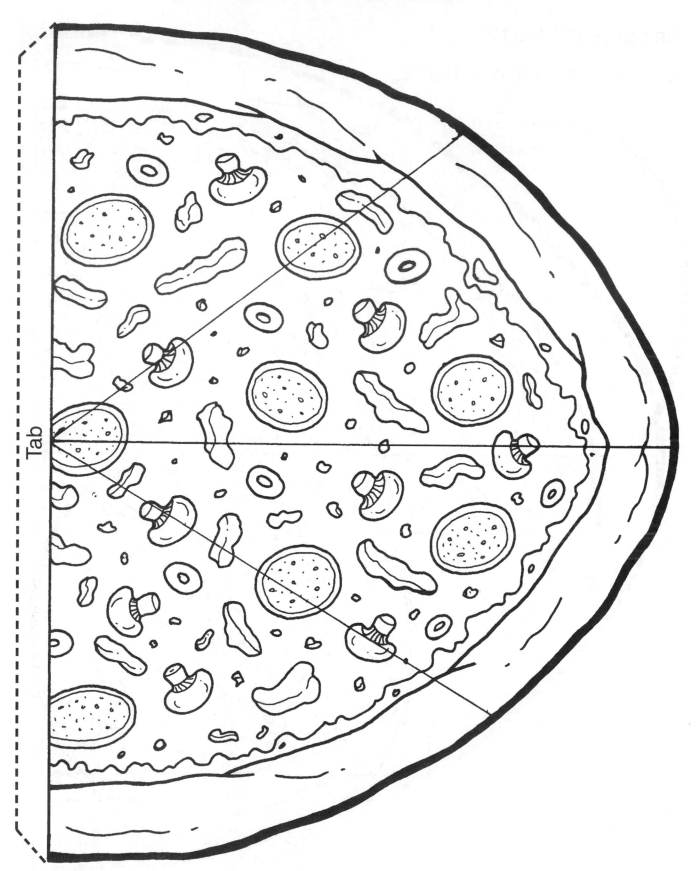

Tab

Apple Fractions

Use pages 213–214.

Apple Fractions *(cont.)*

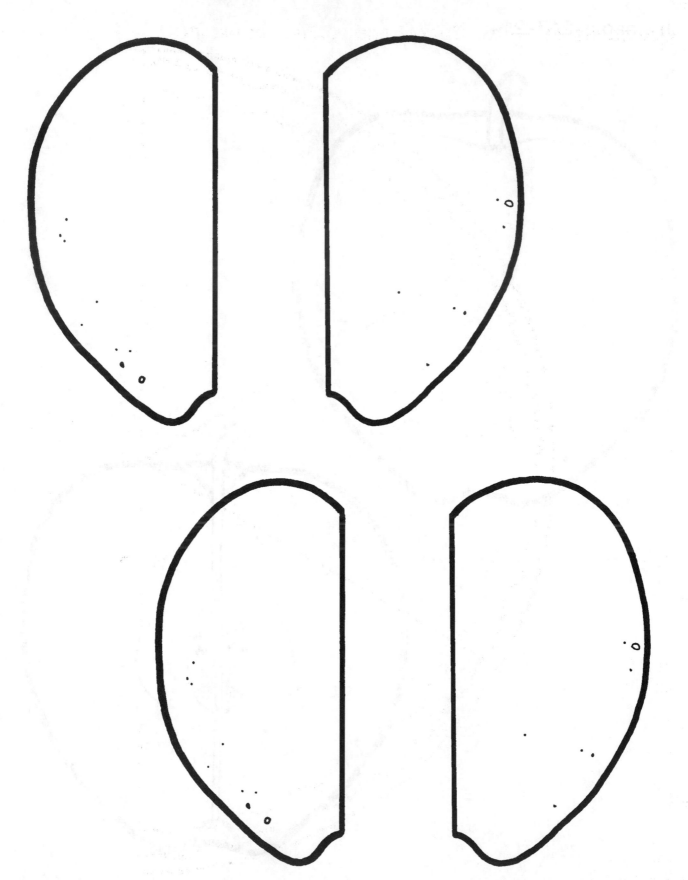

Pie Fractions

Use pages 215–216. Cut out and connect at the tab.

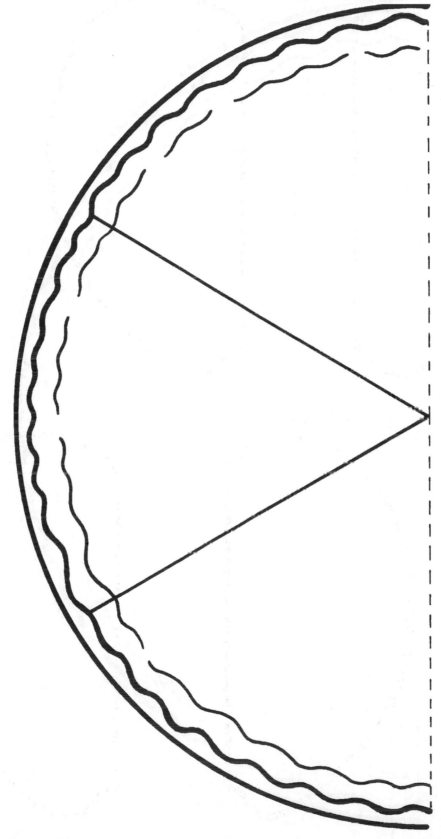

Pie Fractions (cont.)

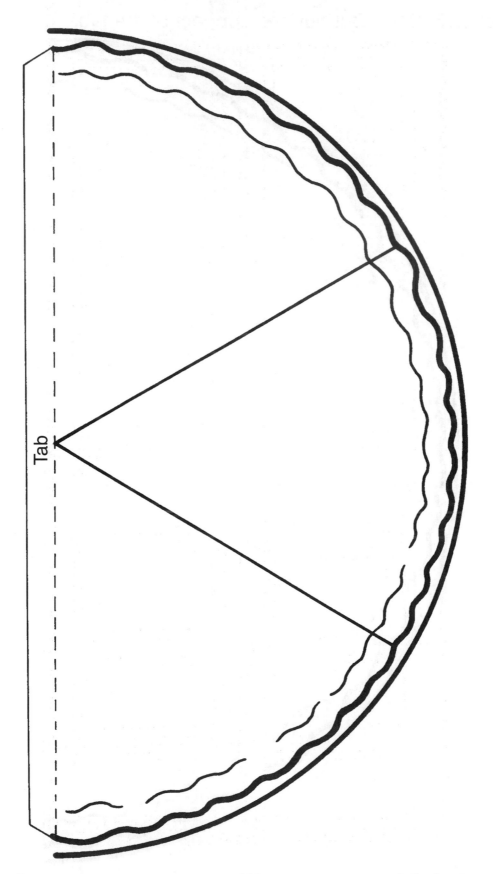

Candy Bar Fractions

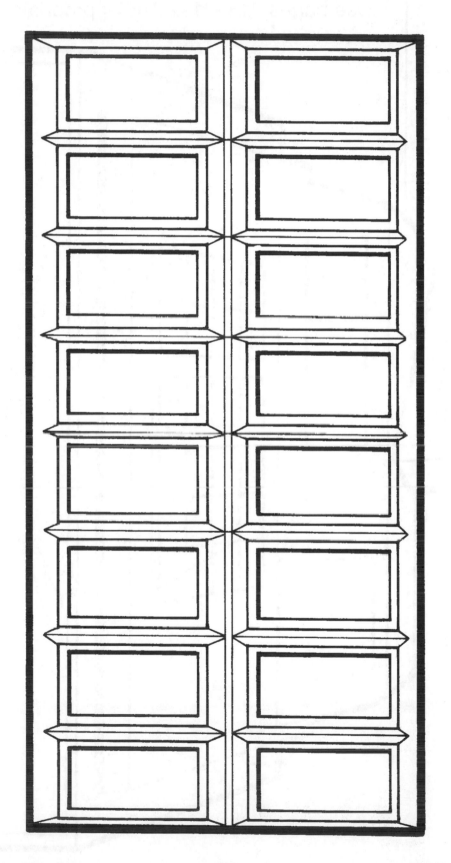

Cash Register

Use pages 218–219. Add appropriate numbers.

Cash Register *(cont.)*

Label drawers with monies being studied. See diagram for drawer placement. Cut out and connect at the tab.

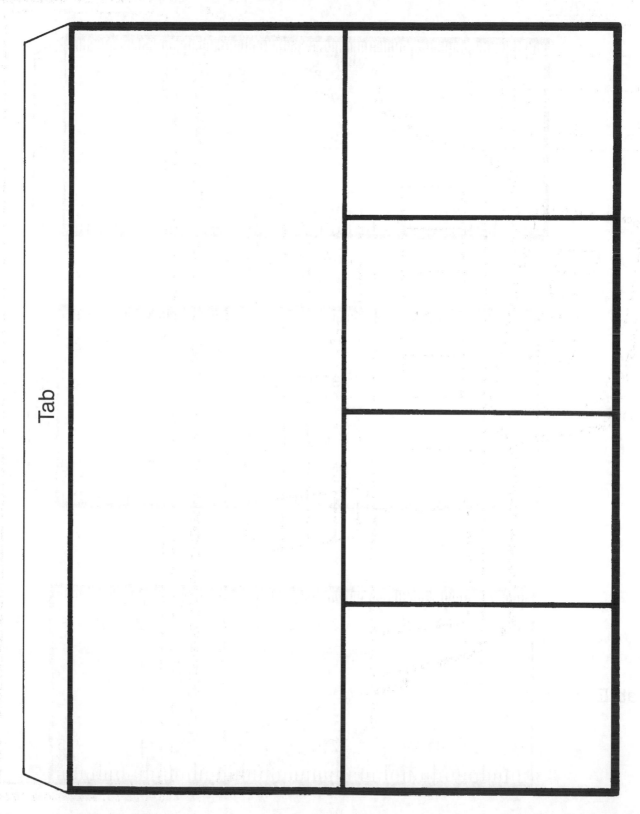

Ruler

Cut out and connect Tabs A and B.

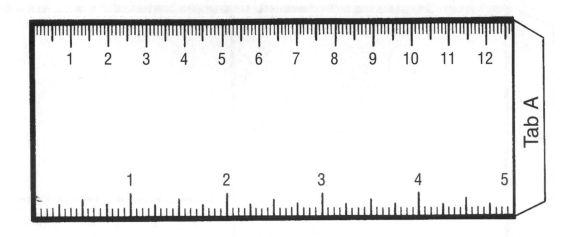

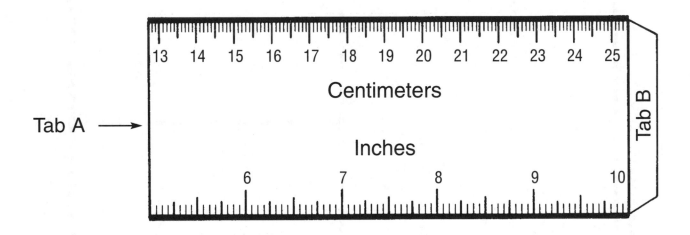

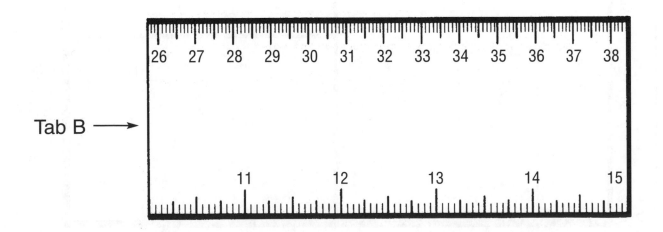

Tape Measure

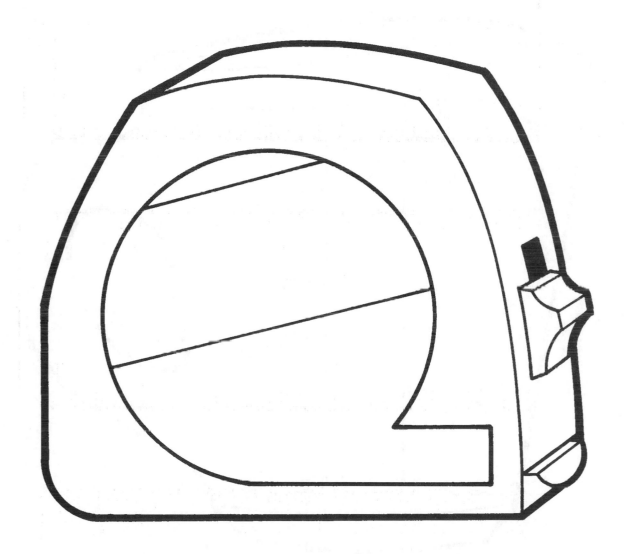

Measuring Cup

240 mL

8 oz.

180 mL

6 oz.

120 mL

4 oz.

60 mL

2 oz.

Pints and Quarts

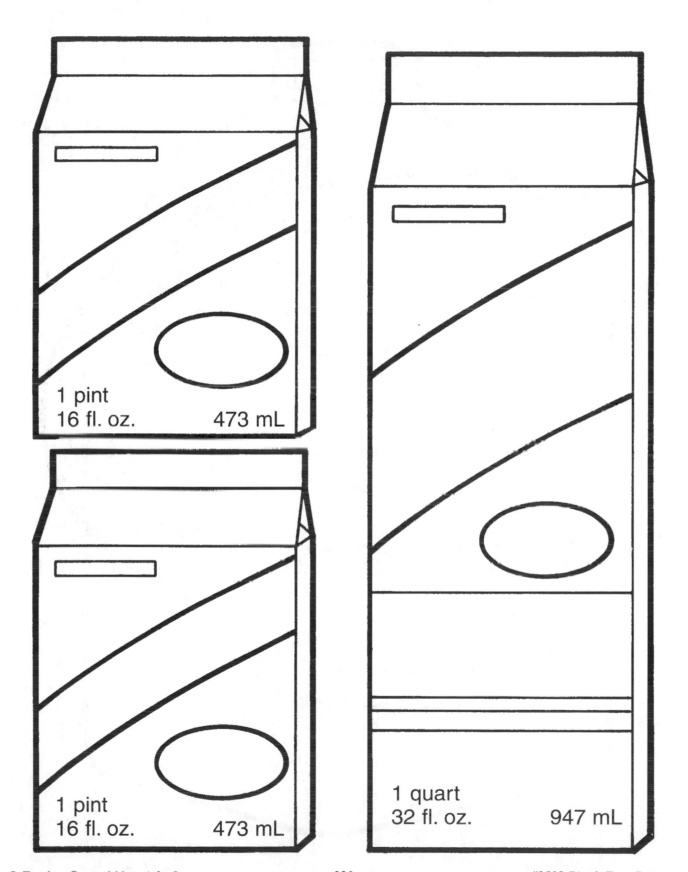

1 pint
16 fl. oz.   473 mL

1 pint
16 fl. oz.   473 mL

1 quart
32 fl. oz.   947 mL

Gallon

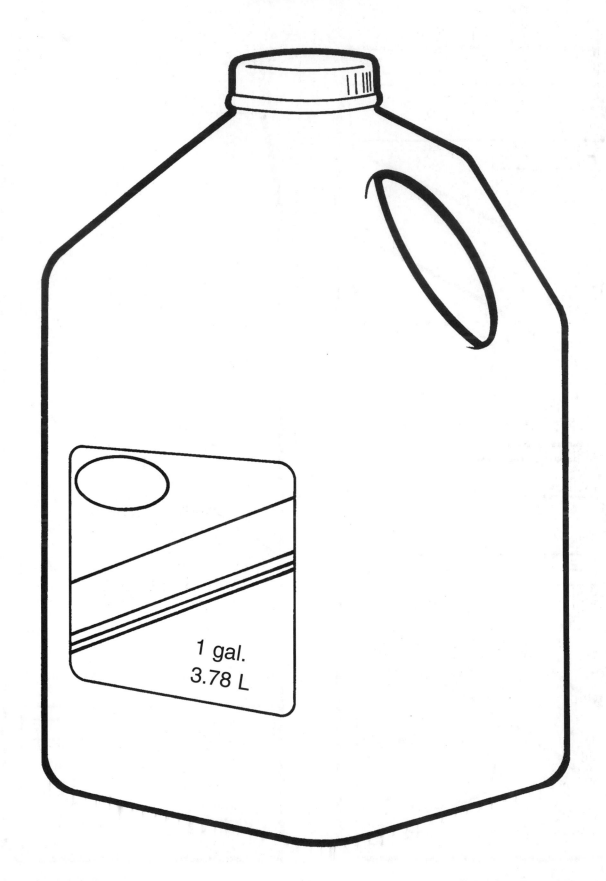

1 gal.
3.78 L